Editorial

The *PN Review* 281 editorial occasioned many responses. Its themes have informed *PN Review* from early on – how writers exist between as well as within languages and dialects. The activity of translation from one language to another, from a given to an acquired dialect, can appear analogous to the initial process of generating experience itself in and as language. Many of us are differently, sometimes conflictedly, alive in a variety of languages. Alive even in *dead* languages, one might say, proving those languages anything but mortal.

Readers can tell by the weight of the issue in their hands that *PNR* 283 is overlength. Yet even despite its portliness, we have had to hold over some items to *PNR* 284. It is not hard to suppose the themes aired here will animate our conversations going further forward, too. Among items to anticipate in *PNR* 284 are Zoë Skoulding's 'Translation Relation', Mary O'Malley's 'Notes from a Native', Michael Edwards's 'Poems from Wivenhoe', Richard Gwyn's 'How I Became a Translator' and Hal Coase's 'San Luigi'.

Readers may also be anxious, turning to the first item of the main text, 'Oan Scots and Respair', to find it actually *in* Scots. It was a deliberate decision to start here. Given our theme – *Between Language* – it seemed salutary to expose monoglot and polyglot readers alike to an initially unfamiliar, even alienating version of our *lingua franca*. Dwelt on (if the reader is a little patient), 'Oan Scots…' provides a compellingly *grounding* experience; it discloses how much more we know and can infer if we persist, make our mouths shape unfamiliar sounds, then listen for the sense which they deliver. Colin Bramwell and I agreed not to add a glossary, inviting readers to 'translate' from the inside. This is remote from 'our accentless inner voice' which Zinovy Zinik evokes in his essay, the voice that does not distract the listener with a specific sound of origin. For most writers, the best auditor is the reader, experiencing writing from the inside. The reader's voice animates the text, not the writer's.

When Gabriel Josipovici read the editorial to *PNR* 281, he sent me an offprint of his 2019 lecture, 'Is there such a thing as a native language', published in *Raritan* and reproduced here with that magazine's kind permission. I shared it with contributors to this issue, at the same time making generally available (by removing the paywall) recent essays from *PNR* that touch on the themes in different ways, specifically Alberto Manguel's *Selbstgefühl* (*PNR* 266) and Stav Poleg *Running Between Languages* (*PNR* 267). I invited reflections, leaving the brief as open as I could.

For this issue, I modified the title of Stav Poleg's essay from plural to singular, 'Between Language', figuratively embedding the preposition in the noun, fragmenting 'Language' like shattering a drop of mercury into droplets which roll apart, then reconfigure. Or drops of dew on a nasturtium leaf. That reconfiguration may be inadvertent; it may be wholly natural. Howard Cooper in his essay 'Ur-Language' reflects on 'the transformative potential of language, well-used': 'We share linguistic worlds with those who preceded us, and I like to think I hear the echoes and reverberations of that archaic mythos in the poetry my father knew by heart but never shared with me.'

Victoria Moul, her imagination and memory charged with English, Latin and much else, is learning Russian. She takes the theme in a direction I would readily follow.

> Speaking another language – indeed, speaking at all – is risky and difficult; it never works perfectly; you can be misunderstood; the pain of incomprehension and imprecision is real; and others might take your words and do wrong by them. But each time we try to reach across that divide, however ineffectually, between the word and its meaning, we are become a *lapis offensionis et petra scandali*, a little incarnation; a moment of grace; and the ruin of the wickedness of the world, in all its awful variety.

This has turned into a rather special 'special issue', touching on matters at the heart of so many writers' cultures, including those of our founding editors, our later contributing and associate editors, and our contributors today.

Letters to the Editor

Mark Dow writes: A quick note on the theme of hymns raised in the editorial to *PN Review* 282. Last month I was in Appleton, Wisconsin, for the memorial service of a friend's mother. My friend's parents were deeply involved in the Korean Methodist church in Wisconsin. When the group started singing I didn't understand what I was hearing. Then I realized some people were singing the hymn in English and others in Korean. (The lyrics sheets were bilingual.) At synagogues I've heard prayers sung in Hebrew and others in English but never at the same time. It was odd and wonderful.

PN Review was deliberately copied into an email that read in part as follows: 'I thought you might be interested to know that I now have over one million pages on Bing. Many published poets have far fewer. I have achieved this with zero help from the British Poetry Establishment. Zilch!'

News and Notes

Forty-six years of *Parnassus* • *PN Review* was sad to miss the public tribute honouring forty-six years of the magazine *Parnassus: Poetry in Review* and its exemplary editor Herb Leibowitz on 30 April at Poets House, New York. *Parnassus*, though slightly junior to *PNR*, always had a bracingly mature feel given the classic format, physical and intellectual weight, variety and style that Herb Leibowitz brought to it, and his minute love and attention, properties of a brilliant and concentrated editor.

Born in 1935, Leibowitz worked as a lecturer and instructor all over New York, including City University, Hunter College and New York University. In 2007, he received the Poetry Foundation's Randall Jarrell Prize for Criticism. He wrote brilliantly on Hart Crane (subject of his doctoral dissertation), William Carlos Williams, and on autobiography. His book *Fabricating Lives: Autobiographical Studies* (published by New Directions) explores the craft and craftiness of the autobiographer, the disclosure and projection, the settling of scores, the *invention* entailed in telling selective versions of the truth. It starts with Benjamin Franklin, and further quarries include Gertrude Stein, Richard Wright and Emma Goldman. Leibowitz is the kindest and most enabling editor I ever encountered, and I raise a grateful glass to him regularly. I was sorry to miss the physical celebration.

Time like a gilded clock • *Jena Schmitt writes*: French poet, essayist and translator Claire Malroux died on 4 February, seven months before her 100th birthday. Born in the Albigeois region, in southwestern France, she spent most of her life in Paris and Cabourg. Malroux was born after the turmoil of the First World War and lived through the Second. Her father died fighting in the Résistance. Describing her writing, Malroux said she 'needed to leave a witness, a witness of my youth and my passage in this world. For people to eventually read after me.' She wrote over a dozen collections of poetry, *La Femme sans paroles* (2006), *Eros* (2006), *Ni si lointain* (2004), *Soleil de jadis* (1998), *Météo Miroir* (2020) and *Reverdir* (2000) among them. Two innovative hybrid texts appeared in 2009 and 2015, *Traces, sillons* and *Chambre avec vue sur l'éternité*, the latter an imagined dialogue with Emily Dickinson, a poet with whom she felt 'a personal affinity'. She translated Dickinson's and Wallace Stevens's complete poems into French, and English-language writers such as Marilyn Hacker, Henri Cole, Derek Walcott, Saul Bellow, H.D., Anne Carson, Charles Simic, Elizabeth Bishop and Elizabeth Barrett Browning, receiving prestigious translation awards such as the Prix Maurice-Edgar Coindreau, the Prix Laure Bataillon and the Chevalier de la Légion d'honneur. In 2020 NYRB Poets published *Daybreak: New and Selected Poems*, translated by Marilyn Hacker. Malroux's poems are as bright and vivid as paintings, and often speak of her family, of past and present overlapping, of mortality, light, loss, gardens, art, music, desire, ageing, History with a capital *H*, and the silent persistence of time that clicks like a gilded clock in the Musée d'Orsay. 'I want to wrench myself out of time's ballast', she wrote in the poem 'Octet Before Winter', which she did again and again through her writing. The American poet Henri Cole, noting her passing, wrote of his friend: 'She promised me she would live to 100, because her work would then be done'.

Playing Bottom • *Michael Schmidt writes*: Clive Wilmer, who died suddenly on 13 March as the result of a stroke, was one of the key contributors to *PN Review* and a defining presence in the magazine from its early issues through 2014. He contributed a series of crucial interviews with poets between 1989 and 1992, several broadcast on Radio 3 and then collected in *Poets Talking* (Carcanet, 1994), including Czesław Miłosz, Charles Causley, Tony Harrison, Les Murray, Donald Davie, Ted Hughes, Patricia Beer, John Heath-Stubbs, P.J. Kavanagh,

Michael Longley and John Peck. He was himself interviewed by Kevin Jackson in 1996. Among his almost 100 contributions were selections of his own poetry, reviews and major essays on figures key to his own writing, including John Ruskin, Thom Gunn and Donald Davie, and brilliant obituary celebrations of Tony Tanner, Alan Stephens, Edgar Bowers and others. He was also a significant translator mainly from the Hungarian in collaboration with his friend George Gömöri.

In the *Guardian* Peter Carpenter celebrated his championing (as editor and lecturer) of Ruskin's work and abiding value. From 2009 he was master of the Guild of St George, 'a national charity "for arts, craft and the rural economy" founded by Ruskin in 1871'. He also stressed his affinities with Thom Gunn, a friend for forty years whose essays and later letters he edited with great tact. He was also deeply engaged by the poetry and prose of Ezra Pound – and Donald Davie. Carpenter reminds us that when he was very young he was a member of the National Youth Theatre, 'playing Bottom alongside Helen Mirren'.

His poems, starting with *Devotions* (1991), were published for many years by Carcanet Press, including a *New and Collected Poems* in 2012. His final book, *Architecture & Other Poems*, will be published by Worple Press later this year.

National Endowment • Donald Trump, the *Washington Post* reported on 3 May, has proposed cancelling the National Endowment for the Arts and Humanities, 'reviving his failed first-term attempts to scrap the grantmaking agencies as he moves to reshape the nation's artistic and cultural landscape'. The NEA and NEH have already cancelled grants and reduced staff in compliance with executive directives. 'The tentative budget plan also targets the Institute of Museum and Library Services and the Corporation for Public Broadcasting.' The NEA was established in 1965, twenty-one years after the British Arts Council. It supports museums, libraries, universities, and public television and radio stations. The 2026 budget proposals require Congressional approval before they can be implemented but anticipation is a powerful censor, as those who live in fear of other kinds of cancellation have learned in recent years. Soon after Trump's plans were published, 'the NEA reportedly rescinded grants for several theatres, citing Trump's artistic priorities', the *American Theatre* magazine reported. At least 1,200 NEH grants have also been discontinued and the NEH has reduced its staffing levels. Money saved is to be spent instead on Trump's plans to create a National Garden of American Heroes for the 2026 Declaration of Independence 250th anniversary celebrations. Congress made sure of the NEA's and NEH's survival last time round. This time their future is less certain.

Between Language

Oan Scots and Respair

COLIN BRAMWELL

A mindin fae bairnheid: waitin aa day fur my posh Kentish kizzens tae win at wir hoose in the north ae Scotland, and the thocht occurrin. *See if thir fae aa the wey doun thir in the sooth ae England, and am fae aa the wey up here, hou are we sposed tae ken the ither's leid? If thir spikkin Inglis, whit dae I spikk?* And keepin that tae myself – kennin in my hairt thir wiss nocht tae fear, bit fearin nanetheless.

It wiss dark bi the time a siller Jaguar announced itsel oan the gravel. Syne I mind kennin ilka ward; and widdershins, bein kent bi thaim and aa. Syne later, wae the lichts oot, sharin my room wae the kizzen I wiss closest tae in age. 'Frazer, see in England, whit d'ye cry the toilet?' And the puir seriousness in his repone. 'In England, we call it *the loo*.'

Etymologically-savvy readers (i.e., maist *PNR* subscribers) wull aye huv jaloused that the ward 'loo' – sae specifically *English* tae Wee Frazer's inchoate mind – is, in point ae fact, French. And nae even Auld, Norman French, bit recent French, fae the lest century. 'Lieux d'aisances'; place of ease. Adoptit bi English sodgers durin the Erst Warld War.

Twas ever thus: the mair forcefully we attribute a ward tae a certain territory or nation, the mair likely wull find that same ward tae hae originatit fae ootlin pairts. In Scots, fur instance, thirs extralinguistic influences pairtit wae Inglis – French, Latin, Auld Norse, Dutch, Greek – houiver, as thae connections were furmed at a time ae greater autonomy for Scots-speakin territories, users ae the Scots leid picked and chose different wards fae the abune. That's hou come, insteid ae followin the Auld Inglis 'crow' – a ward that chimes wae similar constructions in Auld Saxon, Dutch and German – in Scots we hae the 'corbie'; closer tae the French 'corbeau'. A rare example in Scots ae a Romance airt bein chosen ower a Germanic wan.

Of course, ither, native leids aye influenced Scots; Gaelic, Pictish, Cumbric. Bit the noticeably Germanic twang tae Scots can be accoontit fur bi the influence ae Auld Norse; and, due tae the early establishment ae trader burghs wae the Low Countries, Dutch and Middle Low German. In conversation I've hud cause tae descrieve Scots as *mair* Germanic nor Inglis. Goethe oan his deathbed: 'mehr licht', means the exact same in Scots.

I chored that example fae the Scottish-Jewish literary critic David Daiches. And in *Two Worlds,* Daiches's bairnheid memoir, an exceptional correspondence tweesh Scots and Yiddish minority languages is mairked. Daiches descrieves the 'trebblers', itinerant Orthodox Jewish door-tae-door salesmen, livin in the run-doun parts of Edinburgh's Old Town, wha took the Dundee train tae peddle thir wares in the fishin touns ae Fife. Whun these migrants erst arrived in Scotland, they cud aye converse wae Scots-speakers in puir Yiddish, wae gey little meanin tint alang the wey. Ower time thir Yiddish naiturally modified tae accommodate Scots lexis. The resultin dialect wiss, accordin tae Daiches, 'one of the most remarkable ever spoken by man.' 'Aye man, ich hob' getrebbelt mit de five o'clock train', one trebbler would say to another. 'Vot time's yer barmitzvie, laddie?' I was once asked. 'Ye'll hae a drap o' bramfen (whisky). It's Dzon Beck. Ye ken: "Nem a schmeck fun Dzon Beck."' ('Take a peg of John Begg', the advertising slogan of John Begg whisky.)' A century oan, this dialect is lang-deid. Bit whit a wonder it iver existit.

Nae surprises, syne, that in Franz Kafka's weel-kent speech delivered tae introduce a nicht ae Yiddish poetry, mony ae his conclusions aboot Yiddish apply tae Scots. 'Everyone who speaks the German language is also capable of understanding Yiddish. For, seen from a distance, though of course only from a great distance, the superficial comprehensibility of Yiddish is a product of the German language.' Inglis reader – d'ye ken?

Kafka conteenas tae say that it's impossible tae translate Yiddish intae German withoot destroyin the delicate linkages which bind thaim, but aye haud thaim distinct. '*Toit*, for instance, is not the same thing as *tot* (dead), and *blüt* is far from being *blut* (blood).' A gey important pynt, tho *impossible* might be over-eggin it. Certainly the widdershins is possible; German micht be owerset intae Yiddish, and Inglis can, maun, be pit intae Scots.

Why 'maun'? Because in mony cases this airt ae traivel wull be necessary tae appen grund fur the revitalisation ae Scots in general usage. Maist ae my generation ae Scots dinnae spikk the leid, bit as we spikk 'Scottish Standard English', presumably wir somewhaur oan a spectrum, sae we hae the option ae intensifyin wir weys ae spikkin intae fill braid Scots. Wha kens if that'll be the same aye fur future generations, bit. Up tae us.

As a non-native spikker, I'm aye owersettin tweesh Scots and Inglis, and sae I fear the latter'll aye come erst tae me. Bit the mair I yaise Scots, the mair I grant myself permission tae think in the leid and aa, nae jist tae scrieve in it.

Proof's in the bannock. Whun I'm scrievin in Scots, the final product inevitably thumbs its nose tae the airs, graces and rules ae 'standard Inglis'. And nae jist tae RP, bit aye tae the shit solipsism ae American Poststructuralese that's been taught tae my ain generation ae over-unner-educatit poets – and throu which gey mony ae us connive at poetry's worsenin irrelevance tae nonspecialist readers.

Scots winna thole deconstruction; aiblins nae minority leid wull, as thir sheer existence is sufficient challenge tae majority wans. Just yaisin Scots somehou automatically interrogates the verra roots ae Inglis; erodes a boundary tweesh it and its associatit warlds. The Scots linguist Ashley Douglas identifies a spectrum rinnin fae puir Inglis tae braid Scots; maist spikkers are somewhaur in the middle at praisent. Sae Scots gies us writers a slidin scale tae abstract wir Inglis fae the 'standard' variety – in ither wards, a hail clanjamfrie ae weys tae begeck (trick, deceive, disappoint) Teuchter, Belter, 'Northern' and Southron reader alike.

As it's relatively easy tae jalouse, Scots pynts the wey tae aiblins the least fashsome gate tae bilingualism fur Inglis spikkers. Globally, the Scots leid is a muckle stane in the shoe ae ascendant monoglotism.

Spikkin ae which, I'd aye jalouse that it's nae fur nothin wir new-auld cunt-in-chief Donald Trump hus, jist weeks aby, established Inglis as the official leid ae the USA. We aa ken Trump's an autocrat bi nature – that's hou come he prefers the warld tae be rin bi the dictators and ither imperialists he admires – and bi/multilingualism is a naitural threat tae that unintellectual position. Turnin his kintra monoglot allous him fause kiver, ablo which he intensifies his attack oan yir tired huddled masses yearnin tae be free – or free aneuch tae be able tae spikk thir ain tongues elsewhaur.

The neist authoritarian step in Trump's programme wull be tae ettle at bannin thae ither leids fae American public discourse. His team huv aye provided a list ae wards that public institutions, noo bein purged ae 'woke' terminology, shud avoid in public communication. Here's some highlights. *Belong; bias; Black; climate crisis; disability; diversity; equality; ethnicity; female; historically; injustice; LGBT; Native American; oppression; pollution; prejudice; prostitute; racism; segregation; stereotype; trans; victim; woman.*

Ban these wards – ban ony wards – and watch yir kintra git thicker. Bit thon's hou despots attack dissent. It's a lesson that us in linguistically-diverse Europe maun heed. The preservation ae oor tongues isnae a luxury, bit a bulwark anent fause authority, anent tyranny.

Ironic that Trump's ain mither, Mary Anne MacLeod, wiss born intae a croftin family oan Lewis, and sae hud Gaelic as her mither tongue. In Donald's ain backgrund, syne, we huv an immigrant fleein poverty in her hameland. Aiblins Trump's racist invective anent immigrants maun be, tae an extent, self-directit; the naitural result ae Norman Bates levels ae self-loathin. Bit whit a thocht experiment, tae imagine if Mary hud passed oan the Gaelic tae her bairns; whit the psychological impact ae bilingualism micht hae been oan her boy.

Which brings us tae despair. And its forgotten coonterpairt, respair: an auld Inglis ward, noo obsolete, tho Susie Dent's daein her best tae bring it back intae usage. It means 'fresh hope; a recovery from despair'.

I huv foond a bittie respair in the raised consciousness aroond Scots in Scotland at this maument in time; and in the continuance ae a Scots lyric tradition intae oor century. Thirs nae room fur complacency, houiver. The remuival ae important Scots texts fae the Higher curriculum – Lewis Grassic Gibbon's *Sunset Song*, and Rabbie Burns – oan accoont ae the fact that pupils these day dinnae unnerstaund them, feels like wir ettlin oot the rang airt. The possibility that sic writers micht aye be kent bi pupils wha spikk Scots, or somethin close tae it, shud be sufficient evidence tae conteena the noble tradition ae buggin aa Scottish kids tae read texts fae thir ain cultural tradition that'll challenge thaim. My generation ae Scots writers learnt thir tongue throu sic buiks.

The decline ae Shakespeare inwae the Scottish curriculum is also self-defeatin. Tryin tae learn Inglis withoot Shakespeare is like tryin tae learn physics withoot Newton. An alike conclusion can be drawn regardin Scots and Burns. If Scots scrievers were gien a say in the design ae the literary curriculum – an obvious step, bit wan that husnae been made – sic mutilations cud be avoided. Bit the truth is that oor sae-cried nationalist government huv embarrassingly little tae say aboot Scots, or Gaelic for that matter.

Whit a wonder it wud be, fur young Scots tae hae thir ain wey ae talkin (ae bein) validatit ootwae the confines ae the iver-ignored literary sphere. I amna suggestin that we mak owermuckle ae the semantic differences tweesh Inglis and Scots; 'the loo' maun remain as easeful a place in baith leids as in French. Bit a greater awareness ae the spectrum ae speech in Scotland wid be revolutionary fur the nation, as it hus been in wir lyric tradition.

In turn, aiblins it micht be recognised that poetry itsel hus pleyed a muckle role in advancin the cause ae Scots; a role it shudnae huv tae pley bi itself fur much langer. It is time, in ither wards, fur the unacknowledged language legislation ae Scottish poets tae be acknowledged. Upcomin language consultations fae the government micht gie us an opportunity oan that score; as I huv argued elsewhaur, Scots is in a state ae managed decline at praisent. Scots scrievers, in particular, maun shout fae the ruiftaps aboot that the noo. We've nae Trump here tae seelence us, or dictate tae us whit wards we can yaise or no.

Insteid ae bein some variety ae exceptionalist Scottish characteristic, wir bilingualism restores Scottish people – politically-speakin, a nonexistent nation – tae the human commonweal. And the history ae Scots scrievin in the lest century is the story ae that reinstatement; the establishment ae a civic link tweesh poetry and the warld which reads it, hears it – and, in the absence ae organised religion, needs it.

Bilingualism is existential fur a Scottish lyric tradition; and the preservation ae that tradition in Scots letters wull aye be indissowlable wae advancement in the leid. Whit better, final proof can I gie yiz, *PNR* readers, that poetry itself *is* relevant tae the here and noo, despite oor eident, necessary fears that it isna, or winna be in future. Fur noo, as iver, it's aa in hou ye scrieve it. Frost hud it richt: aa the fun's in hou ye say the thing. And thirs yir respair.

Noo, reader, back tae yir Inglis.

from thrums

THOMAS A. CLARK

in mountain top detritus
berries form from clouds
snow crystals melt
into starry saxifrage

.

better than knowledge
than understanding
is lightness
access or ease

.

where drainage is impeded
bright orange racemes
of the bog asphodel
adornment of scarcity
saffron of the poor

.

sad passions pass
slow sad stately
passions pass

.

where land is owned
any wild thing
crossing the land
may be claimed
by right of ownership
any animal
vegetable or mineral
resources claimed
where land is owned
any bright thing

.

fricative affricative
alveolar plosive
rocks in the burn
guttural glottal

.

river gravels
alluvial sediments
merchants masons drovers
passed through the glen
taking their time
here is the sundew
here the marsh orchid
take your time

.

obdurate adherence
of thorns and burrs
of wisps and wasps
ticks and diaspores
to the open vowels

.

if you sit for a while
in the company of an oak
you might begin to reverse
the massive reduction
of the tree to its name

.

in a dappled light
in the clarified air
under birch under pine
reticence as care
shades wintergreen

The Myth of the Native Language

GABRIEL JOSIPOVICI

> I always think that one of the purest emotions is that of the banished man pining after the land of his birth. I would have liked to show him straining his memory to the utmost in a continuous effort to keep alive and bright the vision of his past, the blue remembered hills and the happy highways, the hedge with its unofficial rose and the field with its rabbits, the distant spire and the near bluebell... But because the theme has already been treated by my betters and also because I have an innate distrust of what I feel easy to express, no sentimental wanderer will ever be allowed to land on the rock of my unfriendly prose.

So writes Sebastian Knight, the eponymous hero of Vladimir Nabokov's *The Real Life of Sebastian Knight*, articulating the classic view of the exile's nostalgia for his homeland even as he punctures its sentimentality. But though Nabokov was every bit as hard on sentimentality as the hero of this, the first novel of his to be written in English, he himself was just as nostalgic for the Russia and the Russian language he had lost, even if a little more sophisticated in his rehearsals of it. English, he always felt, was a straightjacket into which he had been forced by history, and while he was proud of the way he had mastered it, he never lost the sense that by having to forgo his native Russian he had been deprived of a tool that allowed him to express the richness and complexity of the world in a way English never would. This had nothing to do with the innate characteristics of the two languages, of course, but rather with the belief that an acquired language can never match a native one.

At the time, 1940, when Nabokov was coming to terms with the sad realization that if, as seemed probable, his fate was to live in England or America for the rest of his life, and that therefore he would have to force himself to write in English, to the eternal impoverishment of his work, a far worse fate was engulfing an eight-year-old Jewish child in central Europe. In a video film by Nurith Aviv, made in 2012 towards the end of his life, the Israeli novelist Aharon Appelfeld explained, very slowly, as the camera panned over a forest:

> I was born in Czernowitz. My mother tongue was German. With my grandparents we spoke Yiddish. With the servants we spoke Ruthenian. Czernowitz was in Romania and the official language was Romanian. When World War II broke out the idyll of speaking Yiddish was shattered in an instant. My mother was killed. I was separated from my father and sent to a camp. I decided to escape. I was blond and looked like a Ukrainian child, and the world of thieves adopted me. In 1946, at fourteen, I immigrated to Israel. I was without parents, without a language. I had so much inside me, so many experiences, that I could not speak. For a long time I was silent. Little by little I acquired Hebrew. It was not a language that grew within me, it was like a duty. And when I began to write other languages sprang up unbidden into my mouth, but I had to repress them if I wanted to write at all.

The camera settles on a small man in a cap, with a round, kindly face and big glasses, standing outside a low house. The voice goes on:

> Every immigrant carries within him two languages. In Israel in those years there was an ideology: Forget the past. Make a new self. German was my native language but it had been contaminated for me forever by what had happened. But Hebrew too was a hard language in my ears, a language of orders, of commands. I studied Yiddish. It was an act of piety for a lost civilization. Today Hebrew is my natural language, but I have to work at it and every day I am afraid I will lose it. So I go on...

One hears it everywhere in the memoirs of German-speaking Jews who survived the war: the Nazis corrupted the German language, after them I can no longer use it. Georges-Arthur Goldschmidt, the French translator of Peter Handke, who was born and grew up in Germany, recalls in his memoir, *The Fist in the Mouth* (*Le Poing dans la bouche*),

> that deadly administrative jargon which had replaced the German language in those years. A jargon made up of words joined together, *Jungvolk* for the members of the Hitler Youth, *Kinderlandesverschickung*, children's summer camps, *Jugendbewegung*, youth movements, and other monstrous verbal constructions of the same sort. It was a language which sat like a weight on one's back, a criminal language that contaminated the entire German language. That icy and artificial Nazi language, we had been obliged to speak it at school, we spoke only of *Fahnenspruch*, the language of allegiance to the flag, of *Volksgemeinschaft*, that ethnic community from which I had been excluded without understanding why.

Undoubtedly true as this is, it must be remembered that a sense of alienation among German-speaking Jews from the only language they had, the feeling that German could not convey what is most meaningful to them, long antedates the Nazi era. On 24 October 1911, Franz Kafka noted in his diary:

> Yesterday it occurred to me that I did not always love my mother as she deserved and as I could only

> because the German language prevented it. The Jewish mother is no 'Mutter,' to call her 'Mutter' makes her a little comic (not to herself, because we are in Germany), we give a Jewish woman the name of a German mother, but forget the contradiction that sinks into the emotions so much the more heavily. 'Mutter' is peculiarly German for the Jew, it unconsciously contains, together with the Christian splendour, Christian coldness also, the Jewish woman who is called 'Mutter' therefore becomes not only comic but strange. Mama would be a better name if only one didn't imagine 'Mutter' behind it.

This was a period in Kafka's life in which he was trying to find his voice as a writer, and thinking and writing with excitement about the Yiddish theatre which had come to Prague with its leading actor Yitzhak Löwy, who had, for him, come to embody true Jewishness. He concludes his remarks on Jews and the German language: 'I believe that it is only the memories of the ghetto that still preserve the Jewish family, for the word "Vater" too is far from meaning the Jewish father.' No wonder his own father, Hermann Kafka, who had struggled his whole life to escape the clammy confines of the ghetto and the shtetl and who was determined that his children should benefit from a good German education and put their shtetl past behind them, was appalled by Kafka's consorting with this Yiddish actor and made his feelings known to his son with the horrifying aphorism, duly noted by Kafka in his diary: 'He who lies down with dogs picks up fleas'.

But that did not deter Kafka; it only added to his guilt at not turning out to be the son his father so desired. Three months later, on 18 February 1912, he introduced an evening of readings of Yiddish literature by Löwy with a passionate, an almost mystical encomium of the Yiddish language. 'Before we come to the first poems by our Eastern Jewish poets,' he begins, 'I should like, ladies and gentlemen, just to say something about how much more Yiddish you understand than you think.' You do not realize it, he goes on, but your relation to Yiddish is one of dread: 'You are so frightened of Yiddish that one can almost see it in your faces'. That, he goes on, is perfectly natural, but it needs to be understood. 'Our Western European conditions,' he proceeds, if we glance at them only in a deliberately superficial way, appear so well ordered; everything takes its quiet course. We live in positively cheerful concord, understanding each other wherever necessary, getting along without each other whenever it suits us, and understanding each other even then. From within such an order of things who could possibly understand the tangle of Yiddish – indeed, who would even care to do so?

After this strange opening he proceeds to give an account of the history and nature of Yiddish, to explain that it is a bastard language, made up of foreign words, that it originated in the period when Middle High German was mutating into Modern High German, and so on. Then he comes to the evening's programme and introduces the poems Löwy is going to read, before returning to his opening theme: you may think you don't know Yiddish, you may be a little afraid of it even, but 'there are active in yourselves forces that enable you to understand Yiddish instinctively'. If you push it away from you, it will not give itself to you,

> but if you relax, you suddenly find yourselves in the middle of Yiddish. But once Yiddish has taken a hold of you and moved you – and Yiddish is everything, the words, the Chassidic melody, and the essential character of this Eastern Jewish actor himself – you will have forgotten your former reserve. Then you will come to feel the true unity of Yiddish, and so strongly that it will frighten you; yet it will no longer be fear of Yiddish but of yourselves. You would not be capable of bearing this fear on your own, but Yiddish instantly gives you... a self-confidence that can stand up to this fear and is even stronger than it is. Enjoy this self-confidence as much as you can! But then, when it fades, tomorrow or later – for how could it last, fed only on the memory of a single evening's recitations – then my wish for you is that you may also have forgotten the fear. For we did not set out to punish you.

What an extraordinary little speech this is. Almost evangelical in its uplift and earnestness, yet not without humour either, and of course about much more than just language. Like Appelfeld a century later, Kafka sees the access to Yiddish as a return, for Jews, to their roots. *This* is their native language, not the German they learned at school, and by rediscovering it they will rediscover their *real* selves. The German-speaking Jew, for Kafka, is exiled from his native country, which is the country of Yiddishkeit. For Appelfeld things are more complicated: German, the language he grew up speaking, has been irrevocably tainted by the Nazis, but in any case now he has had to learn another alien language, *ivrit*, the modern Hebrew of the state of Israel. In this language, he feels, he will have to find ways of recalling the lost, the missing, the Edenic language, or at least exploring the ways that language, together with culture, was destroyed – by the Nazis, but also, for Appelfeld as for Kafka, by the desire of assimilated Jews before the coming of the Nazis to deny and repress that native language – the language of the grandparents, as he puts it.

As we have seen with the example of Nabokov, however, this is not a specifically Jewish story. Is it even a twentieth-century story? So far my examples suggest that it is, but I want now to introduce another, complicating example, an example not from the twentieth or even the nineteenth century, but from the thirteenth and fourteenth. I am referring to Dante.

Dante is normally seen as representative of the High Middle Ages, just as Shakespeare is of Elizabethan and Jacobean England and Goethe of the Germany at the cusp of the eighteenth and nineteenth centuries. If Kafka is sometimes invited to join them, then it is only as the representative figure of our broken and fragmented modern world. Dante, Shakespeare and Goethe, on the other hand, are seen as supremely self-confident, their individual genius both drawing on and contributing to the self-confidence of the societies they represent.

Yet Dante and Kafka are curiously aligned in their attitude to language.

Dante was not only the greatest poet of the Middle Ages, he was also the first comparative philologist. His early Latin treatise *De vulgari eloquentia* is an attempt to chart the relation to each other of the burgeoning Romance vernaculars: French, Provençal and Italian. He undertakes this task for a very personal reason. Throughout the Middle Ages Latin had been seen as the language of courts, of the law, and of high literature. The people could produce ballads and lyrics in the vernacular, but for the serious poet there was only one language, Latin. Besides, if you wrote in the vernacular you would be writing in a language that was constantly changing, as well as in one that could only be understood by a small minority, those who spoke Provençal, for example; whereas if you wrote in Latin you would not only be following in the steps of Virgil, you would also be reaching a European audience, and you would ensure that the language you wrote in would never change. How was the poet who saw himself as the descendant of Virgil and a spokesman for Christian Europe to write in any language other than Latin?

And yet against this perfectly reasonable argument for Latin there raged another in Dante's breast. In both *De vulgari eloquentia* and his unfinished philosophical treatise, the *Convivio*, he makes a powerful case for the primacy, not just in time but in importance, of the native language, what he calls the language of *mamma* and *babbo*. Were it not for this language, the language learned at the mother's breast, he argues, perhaps tongue in cheek, my parents would not have been able to converse, and if they had not been able to converse they would not have discovered they were in love and so they would not have married and I would not have been born. The native language, he goes on in the *Convivio*, verging on blasphemy in his excitement, is like a familiar house to be entered with pleasure, like a table laid for a banquet, a new life, a new sun; it is the fire that warms our frozen limbs, it is the bread of life.

Dante was an innovator here as in so much else. It is, he began to think, not only possible for the ambitious national poet to write in his native language, it is imperative that he do so. Though Petrarch, fifty years after Dante, would write *his* epic in Latin, the drift of history was with Dante – no one reads Petrarch's epic, *Africa*, written in Latin hexameters, though Petrarch's lyrics, written in the vernacular, are still very much alive. This is not just because no one reads Latin anymore; it is – and this is the real thrust of Dante's argument – because only by opening yourself up to your native language can you open yourself up to what are the deepest roots of your being. Therefore, to write in Latin is to cut yourself off from the wellsprings of your creativity.

This is all well and good, but it doesn't answer the question of the limited reach of a work written in, say, Provençal or Tuscan. Perhaps more important, it doesn't answer the question whether, since vernacular languages change in time, a work written in one of them is doomed to extinction. The words the poet seeks to align, if he turns his back on Latin,

> strain,
> Crack and sometimes break, under the burden,
> Under the tension, slip, slide, perish,
> Decay with imprecision, will not stay in place,
> Will not stay still,

as Eliot, Dante's modern heir, was to put it in his own meditation on this issue, the *Four Quartets*.

There are no 'answers' to such questions – only the individual quests of individual writers to resolve the issue for themselves, from the time of Dante to our own. Dante had, from the beginning, been recognized in his circle of Florentine poets as special. His early collection of love lyrics to the woman he called Beatrice, organized into a narrative by means of linking prose passages and named *La Vita Nuova, The New Life*, had at once marked him out as an artist of superabundant talent and ambition. But he was dissatisfied with what he was doing, and in the following years sought to understand the nature of his gift and to clarify how best to use it, by undertaking a series of prose works of a philosophical, critical and political nature. Some of these were written in Latin – his treatise on language, *De vulgari eloquentia*, his essay on good governance, *De Monarchia* – and some in the vernacular, such as the *Convivio*, ostensibly a gloss on a series of his own poems but in effect a philosophical meditation on many subjects. Most of these remained unfinished. And the reason for this, he began to understand, was that he had to start with what he felt, not what he could understand, and gradually work towards the clarification of those feelings. Thus, he came to realize, only poetry, and only an extended narrative poem, would truly satisfy him. And so he embarked on the *Commedia*, the story of a man lost in a dark wood in the middle of his life. This would be a poem that was not only written in the vernacular, but also would not avoid the common and the childish – the speech of *mamma* and *babbo* – and would integrate this with the most complex and exalted language. And in so doing, it would forge a vernacular that would be capable of withstanding the changes that are a necessary part of all languages, not by acting as a bulwark against such change, as Latin had been, but by somehow being flexible enough to accept and encompass it. A quixotic ambition, perhaps, but one that has been vindicated by history. Though speakers of Italian may find Dante a little harder to read than the latest novel in their language, he still remains, with a slight effort, perfectly readable, for he was the forger of modern Italian.

Let us try to understand a little better what Dante's achievement in the *Commedia* implies, which is another way of saying: let us try and understand what the *Commedia* is saying, for the argument of the narrative and the triumph of language go together. As he emerges from the dark wood, the protagonist finds that a guide has been sent to help him on his journey, one who is none other than his great mentor, the Latin poet Virgil. He is guided by Virgil down the spiral of the first canticle, the *Inferno*, where he meets a great variety of sinners, those who never repented even at the last minute. 'As I was then so am I now' is the burden of their refrain, however diverse the stories they have to tell.

Dante is often moved by these stories and has to be pushed on by Virgil towards his destination, which is first down to the pit of hell and then up to the top of Mount Purgatory, where Beatrice will take over and guide him through the spheres of the heavens. He is sorry for these people, and they are sorry for themselves. Nostalgia is the prevalent emotion here, but as we see it at work in the terraces of hell we realize both how natural it is to human beings and how dangerous – for these people are in love with their former selves, and this is in a sense why they are in hell in the first place: they have never been able to let go of their older, sinful ways. What the pilgrim – and, through him, the reader – has to learn is that we must both accept our childish selves *and* learn how to put them by, if we are to develop our full potential. This is a hard lesson, but it is also a joyful one. Dante is the great poet of joy, which is what distinguishes him from the theologians whose works form the backbone to his thinking – Thomas Aquinas, St. Bonaventure, St. Augustine. Any development, too, the poem teaches us, is always tentative, and never more so than in the final beatific vision. This we can never grasp, only follow that journey towards it, not because it is forever out of reach but because it is ever out of our powers to formulate it.

So as we approach the end he warns us: 'Now will my speech fall more short, even in respect of that which I remember, than that of an infant who still bathes his tongue at the breast' (che d'un fante/che bagni ancor la lingua alla mamella). He sees, or thinks he remembers seeing, the image of the Trinity within the pure circle, but then, he confesses for one last time, 'my wings were not sufficient for that, save that the mind was smitten by a flash wherein its wish came to it. Here power failed the lofty fantasy; but already my desire and my will were revolved, like a wheel that is evenly moved, by the love which moves the sun and the other stars.' Even the syntax keeps us wheeling, for we think at first that the subject is 'my desire' only to find at the last that it is in fact 'love', as those key words, played with and worked on throughout the length of the poem, *amore* and *muovere*, to love and to move, appear for one last time:

> ma già volgeva il mio disio e'l velle,
> come rota ch'igualmente è mossa,
> l'amor che move il sole e l'altre stelle.

Thus ends this extraordinary poem, which began in a way we can all understand, with a man waking up alone, in the middle of his life, lost in a dark wood, only to arrive at this exalted place. In the course of it Dante has touched on just about every aspect of fourteenth-century life and the human psyche both then and now. Like Nabokov and Appelfeld, Dante was an exile – not, it is true, from his native language, but from the city that had given meaning to his life. In his exile he came to understand that there will always be a homeland and a language of babyhood to which we long – with good reason – to return, that this longing must not be brushed aside as sentimental, but it must not be indulged in either; rather, it must be harnessed to something which lies ahead, which has to be worked for rather than longed for, and he, the poet, the *poietes*, the *maker*, does indeed work for it – and for us.

What he does, in the course of this poem, in effect, is to make us understand that that elusive 'native language' is perhaps not so much something that we must forever seek to return to, but that it is rather where we must seek to arrive. And that, we will see, is precisely the lesson that my three exemplary modern writers, in their different ways, also come to understand. But before I return to them I want to introduce a bit of personal history.

The myth of the native language is not merely a question of academic interest to me. For just as Nabokov, Appelfeld and Kafka each had good reason to lament the loss of this language, so I have had good reason to doubt its validity. To explain, I was born in Nice in the south of France to Jewish parents who both came from families settled in Egypt. Very nice, you might say, and so it would have been had the year not been 1940. Anyway, we survived the war, and at its end my mother returned with me to Egypt where I attended an English school before, at fifteen, going to England to finish my schooling and go to university. Eventually I got a job teaching English and comparative literature at the newly formed University of Sussex, where I remained for the course of my working life.

So what does that make me? I have an English passport and I write in English, but I don't feel particularly English and, like Appelfeld, I realize I have only a very frail hold on the English language. I was born in France and only spoke French till I was five, but I don't feel in the least French or have any nostalgia for the French language. I did most of my schooling in Egypt, but in those adolescent years I always felt that I was a stranger in the country, with only a slight command of Arabic. In my thirties, like so many people, I began to be conscious of my roots and learned enough Biblical Hebrew not to feel a complete fraud when I started to teach a course at Sussex on The Bible and English Literature. I eventually wrote a book on the Bible as narrative. I have none of the nostalgia of Kafka and Appelfeld for a lost world of Yiddishkeit. Indeed, it seems as alien – though fascinating – to me as the world of Englishness that I imbibed from my childhood reading of the Just William and Biggles books.

To me, then, the idea of a maternal language, learned at the mother's knee and as life-giving as the Eucharist is to the Christian, is completely alien. As is the nostalgia of Nabokov for his native Russian and of Kafka and Appelfeld for a Yiddish that was the language of their grandparents. Am I an aberration then? Am I the last person who should be writing about the subject? Fortunately for me, there is another writer whose upbringing mirrors mine and who has articulated this condition better than I ever could, and that is the French philosopher Jacques Derrida. In the slim book he has devoted to the subject, a book with the typically obscure title of *The Monolingualism of the Other*, Derrida explains how he grew up in Algeria before the war, French speaking but with a strong sense of not belonging to France, unable to speak the Arabic of those who surrounded him, aware of not being a Catholic or a Muslim but a

Jew, yet ignorant of both Hebrew and Jewish tradition. This condition of being outside everything – outside France and the French language, outside Algeria and the Arab language, outside Judaism and its languages – was the mainspring, the book suggests, for his lifelong attitude of confrontation with French culture, French philosophy and French education, even as he had no wish to substitute *something else* for it – Yiddishness, Judaism and so on. This is the reason, perhaps, for the development of his critical spirit and for his idcas about deconstruction, which is simply the attempt to dethrone essence from its place in our culture – the essence of language, of culture, of human beings. An attempt he has carried through on every single topic he has been faced with and that, in this book, he carries out against the notion of the native language.

'I have but one language,' Derrida repeats throughout this book, 'and it is not my own.' We do not *have* a language, he insists, we *speak* it. The first language does not exist, he argues, it is a lure and a temptation. In one sense, of course, he is plainly wrong: Nabokov had a first language, which, he felt, had been taken from him by the Revolution. Dante had a first language; the question was whether he had to reject or embrace it if he wanted to be a major poet. But perhaps Derrida's peculiar position, more radically alienated from *any* language than even Kafka and Appelfeld, allowed him to see something that the others had only intuited. And perhaps that is true for me as well.

It remains for me to sketch in how the modern writers I began with themselves came to recognize the truth of these claims, even if they never articulated them – indeed, even if they went on mourning the loss of the native language to the end of their lives, as they all did, in their different ways.

Appelfeld's best novels explore what happens when the Jews of Europe turned their backs on their Jewish roots in the mistaken belief that they would be able to blend in more easily with their hosts, or when the Israelis decided that they must ape the physical fitness and disdain for the intellect of the Nazi and Communist regimes they had fled, if they were to prosper in their new home. He shows, in a novel like *The Healer*, how those who sought, in the thirties, to heal their ills by a return to the pure life of ancient Jewish communities were whistling in the dark as much as those who turned their backs in disdain on such communities. In other words, he uses fiction to sketch in a lost wholeness only by showing people who have, for one reason or another, lost it, never by unambiguously glorifying it. His work may be a moving epitaph on European Jewry, but it triumphs precisely because it recognizes it is an epitaph.

The case of Nabokov is a little different. As Michael Wood pointed out in his fine book on the novelist, Nabokov always had a tendency to be precious, perhaps even self-satisfied. He knew from the start that he was something extraordinary, a magician of language almost unrivalled in the modern era. But that leads, in his early Russian novels as in his late novels written in an English he by then felt he had wholly mastered, to a kind of narcissism: capable of creating whole worlds out of words, he ceases to look at the world but looks, preeningly, only at what he has made. The exception to this are the novels he wrote as he was struggling to write in English, to master English – *The Real Life of Sebastian Knight, Pnin, Lolita*. This last, it has been said, is the record of Nabokov's love affair with the English language. It could perhaps more accurately be called his unrequited love affair with the American way of life and with American English. With the popular success of *Lolita* he was able to retire back to the old world and spend his last years in a grand Swiss hotel.

Lolita is a tragedy, and what it describes is the impossibility of holding on to that of which you dream – a young woman, a language. It is also a novel of wonder: it is the otherness of the young woman, of the language, that is both the source of wonder and of frustration. The book opens with Humbert mouthing the syllables of his beloved's name: 'Lo-lee-ta: the tip of the tongue taking a trip of three steps down the palate to tap, at three, on the teeth, Lo.Lee.Ta.' The tragedy, for Humbert, for Lolita, comes from his trying to realize in actual life the sensation of pure joy that saying the name creates inside his mouth.

Beckett, Nabokov's contemporary, was more clear-eyed about the issue. Unlike the other writers I have invoked, he was an exile who chose to leave his native country and his native language precisely because he obscurely felt that attachment to it would destroy him, as a man and as a writer. In *Krapp's Last Tape*, his most autobiographical work, he too has his hero turning a word voluptuously over in his mouth. But that word is 'spool' – the reel of tape he puts in his machine which will play back to him his thoughts, recorded in past years. 'Spooool,' he utters, drawing the vowel out as long as he can, 'spooool.' And it does not escape the constipated speaker, or the audience of a play called *Krapp's Last Tape*, that the word is only one letter away from 'stool'. You think you are coming here to have an insight into the truth of life, Beckett seems to be saying to the audience, well, here it is, life is *crap*, and any attempt to express that crap is crap. Yet he loves the crap, he cannot give it up. So he has to find ways of both going on speaking and destroying what he is saying even as he speaks.

Let me end with a little story Kafka wrote in his middle period, after the horrors of *Metamorphosis* and before the bleakness of late stories like 'The Hunger Artist'. This is the period when he seems to have come to terms with the fact that we have longings which can never be assuaged; we cannot go back and we cannot go forward and upward. What we can do is articulate this situation, and that brings a modicum of peace. Instead of dreaming of a Yiddishness which would lift him into a radiant world quite other than that of his sordid existence with a brutal father and an acquiescent mother, he writes, in 'A Report to an Academy', about an ape who, captured in the African forests, understands that his only hope of a decent life lies in his ability to master the language of his captors. Here he is then, at the height of his fame, lecturing to the academy about his life.

'Honoured Members of the Academy!' he begins. 'You have done me the honour of inviting me to give your Academy an account of the life I formerly led as an ape. I regret' he goes on, 'that I cannot comply with your request to the extent that you desire. It is now nearly five years since I was an ape, a short space of time, perhaps, but an infinitely long time to gallop through at full speed.' But when he does begin he is quite clear as to what was involved: 'I could never have achieved what I have done had I been stubbornly set on clinging to my origins, to the remembrances of my youth. In fact, to give up being stubborn was the supreme commandment I laid upon myself; free ape as I was, I submitted myself to the yoke. In revenge, however, my memory of the past has closed the door against me more and more.' And this magnificent opening paragraph ends: 'To put it plainly: your life as apes, gentlemen, in so far as something of that kind lies behind you, cannot be further removed from you than mine is from me. Yet everyone on earth feels a tickling at the heels; the smallest chimpanzee and the great Achilles alike.'

Though only two or three years have passed, how far we are from Kafka's impassioned plea to the audience at Löwy's Yiddish evening to recognize the Yiddish in themselves. There is here a realism no less painful for being, at this stage in the lecture, expressed so humorously. But by the end the cost of the transformation is made plain, and it is all the more heartrending for being expressed so coolly and precisely in Kafka's mellifluous German:

> Nearly every evening I give a performance, and I have a success which could hardly be increased. When I come home late at night from banquets, from scientific receptions, from social gatherings, there sits waiting for me a half-trained little chimpanzee and I take comfort from her as apes do. By day I cannot bear to see her, for she has the insane look of the bewildered, half-broken animal in her eye; no one else sees it, but I do, and I cannot bear it. On the whole, at any rate, I have achieved what I set out to achieve. But do not tell me it was not worth the trouble. In any case, I am not appealing for any man's verdict, I am only imparting knowledge, I am only making a report. To you also, honoured Members of the Academy, I have only made a report.

Poems

EUGENE OSTASHEVSKY

Two Hearts

Petersburg, eater of Mariupol, where are your speakers of Greek.

Where is the poet Georgis Kostoprav. Where are the schoolteachers.

Where are the proofreaders of *Kolekhtivistis*, who bravely fought the deriders of dialect,
the proofreaders of *Kommunistis.*

Where are the actresses of the Greek Theater, who led country audiences in Ukrainian and
Greek sing-alongs to bolster the friendship of peoples.

Where is the collective farmer Popov, who translated Gogol's *Inspector-General* in the
shadow of his tractor for the benefit of fellow collective farmers.

Is he contributing to the humus-rich soil with the rest of them, their skulls smashed by bullets
entering from the back, their hands tied.

Are your hands tied, Petersburg.

You have smashed the dome of the Greek Church on one of your Soviet streets with a demolition ball
entering from the back, and blocks of masonry collapsed on people seeking safety.

Get glasses, cultural capital, you cannot read the word *children*.

You have bombed a maternity ward to make a clearing for a concert hall, since the
concert hall is the temple of art and art demands sacrifices.

In your own immortal work of art, a dog recognizes a park, though the trees have been gouged out,
and the place where they rustled covered over with asphalt.

Still the dog lifts its leg in the air, because it is still free to do so, since its legs are still untied,
its skull is still intact, its mouth is yet to turn to rot in order that it contribute to culture.

So it can still tell what lies under the parking lot, Petersburg. You have eaten your brother or rather,
as you put it, your sister.

What have you done with the speakers of Ukrainian. What have you done with the speakers of Russian.

17 December 2022

Falling Sonnets

I.

Photographs of young women who recently have been murdered. Goodbye, young women.

We have nothing to say to you. The sun is the same.

Others are now being murdered because you have been murdered. It's like Ancient Greece.

It's automatic. May you rise into chariots in pairs.

One of you shall be the driver, the other the hero.

One of you shall hold the reins, the other two arms of bronze and an oxhide shield.

O young women who have recently been murdered. Please put Corinthian safety helmets over your heads.

Please drive away in your chariots. The blood smear shall remain on us.

Who are the us. We are not the old people left murdered in bathrooms and living rooms.

We are not the young men whose bodies remain on the shoulders of roads. The sun is still the same.

Some of them still have their arms in a holding pattern. They are cradling their imaginary guns.

The imaginary guns are to be cradled the same way as the young women are to be cradled.

The imaginary young women are to be cradled into sleep. They are not heroically to be held in our arms by us.

Who are the us. We are not the children still held heroically hostage in underground cages.

15 October 2023

II.

This war has been made public. Everyone's invited.

The protagonists are wearing balaclavas. Canons are to the right of them.

They drive into the valley of the shadow of death. The sun is in shadow.

The sun is a bloody ring. The finger has been cut off.

We have raped the sun and then cut off its indexing finger.

We have also decapitated the satellites: sun cut off head.

A new Apollo rules over us now. We must change our lives.

We must become strongmen: string, strang, strung. We dig it and we dig it.

We are singing dithyrambs as we ride into the shadow of death, valley of.

We have cast the valley into ad shows. We are the counter casters.

Our encounters are chaste. We have strewn rapeseed over the sun.

We have cut off its tender rays tentacles. It has lost the capacity to feel.

We are the sons of the sun. Our mother found us revolting.

Because this war has been made public the sun is a red brown smear on sweatpants. Everyone's invited.

16 October 2023

III.

How are your deaths to be measured. What is the unit of measurement.

Are we to measure your deaths by other deaths. What ratio is rational.

Or are we to measure your deaths by an act of identification. Who checks whose identification.

How often are we to pass into your deaths. Is it as often as we are not to pass into other deaths.

Are we to pass again into the resistant Zion of the sand grain.

Are we to pass into the skeletal building manufactured from fireproof materials. Do fireproof materials prove a fire.

Are we to enter the blackened trunks of the armature in an imperfect circle of crushed concrete.

Behold these fallen petals of concrete. It is the greyscale cherry blossom festival of concrete. Proponents of abstraction raise their brows at it, for everything must fall.

For they say to one another, The origin of the abstract is the economy.

The origin of the abstract is the economy of cognition. Cognition is an induction engine.

It does not care for the concrete. Or rather, it cares for the concrete only inasmuch as it may be poured around an armature to manufacture a wall but not for the concrete as such.

The word 'concrete', a suspicious word. Like other emotionally rich words it may be converted into an arm, to pick up things. An arm is a utensil.

Who shall lay down whose utensils, you first, no you first. Who shall enter a concrete room when out of Zion shall pour forth instruction. Is not concrete soundproof.

Did he just say, let us beat words into workshares. I believe he said that for he is the god of economy, an abstract and a laissez-faire god.

17 November 2023

Running towards My Childhood

STAV POLEG

There are so many ways to leave a country. Some leave after years of hesitations but keep coming back. Many are forced to flee. Others never really leave, forming their own expat communities wherever they find themselves. And then, there are those – forever outsiders in their own country – who feel an odd sense of relief by finally leaving and becoming official outsiders – foreigners – in a different land. When I left Israel, I slammed the country's door with such force, you could hear the mountains shaking and the waves of the Mediterranean crashing on the shores in response. I didn't want to look back or take anything with me apart from my guitar and a few favourite clothes. All I wished was to go as fast and as far as I could, and this, to an extent, included leaving the only language I could speak. Or at least, that's how it felt then. Because there was another small thing I slipped in my suitcase before I left, and on the night of 7 October 2023 – almost twenty years to the day since I moved to the UK – I urgently needed to find it. Suddenly, it became my most treasured possession: a picture of me and my best friend, aged four, sitting with my cat on the concrete path in Kibbutz Be'eri, our childhood home.

*

In 2022, I wrote an essay for *PN Review*: 'Running Between Languages'. It was written shortly after the publication of my debut poetry collection. The fact was that it was only after the book was published that it dawned on me that I wrote a book in English, a language I could hardly speak when I arrived in the UK. Of course, I was aware that I'd been attempting to write in English as a foreign language, but I always hesitated to dwell on it, for two main reasons. First, I simply wanted my poetry to be judged on its own merit. Second, I've always believed that when it comes to poetry writing, what's really difficult is the act of writing itself. Which language one chooses to use is surely secondary. And while I still find writing in English a daily challenge, it is only difficult in the technical sense. Creatively, it has always felt utterly and entirely freeing.

Still, I wrote the essay as a way to understand why, even when my English was so weak, I attempted to experiment with it, just three months after arriving in the UK. Something unexpected happened while writing that essay: I found myself going back to my early childhood years and the way I struggled with language at that time. It was a painful experience: I thought I'd managed to leave my childhood behind, only to discover the obvious: that I had always carried it with me, no matter which language I used. Looking back now, I realise that I wrote the essay with a deep sense of anger. But what I have discovered in the short time that has passed since writing it, is that it is easier to feel angry towards a place that exists. What happened on 7 October unleashed the deepest feelings of grief, longing, despair and sadness that flowed and pulsated in such force and intensity, they formed new rivers that took with them everything I thought I'd known – about myself, about the people around me, and about the multitude ways we struggle to live in and outside of language.

*

A few months ago, I met a Ukrainian scholar over coffee, and we talked about poetry. She couldn't understand how I was able to create in a language that is not my first tongue. For her, the thought of not writing poetry in Russian – her mother tongue – was inconceivable: she felt it was the only language in which she would ever be able to express herself in each miniscule gesture and detail. Talking to her, it struck me that I never felt I had one language in which I could express my 'truest, deepest self'. No matter which language I use, I often struggle to find precise connections between words and reality, and I almost always feel, during one conversation or another, that what I say out loud is not nearly as accurate as what I wish I could have expressed: it is a constant struggle against what feels like the limits of language, a constant failure.

Perhaps there is something about early traumatic events that creates a fracture between reality and language. It's as if, as a child, you experience some kind of an earthquake, or a series of earthquakes, that cause the words around you to separate, brutally, from the material objects they were integral to only a few seconds before. Suddenly, language fails to carry what happens around you, because the impact from the eruption blew the words away and all you are left with is a material world that is not only shattered but has lost all meaning.

There is a map of my childhood I keep trying to draw: a small, private space of images and words. By the time I turned five, I had already experienced several losses: a series of personal earthquakes. There are so many things I only half remember. But what I know is that from a very early age I was always acutely aware that there was some kind of a gap between language and the world around me: a fissure that kept changing – at times becoming deeper or shallower – but never completely healing.

Perhaps if language always feels difficult, it doesn't seem like such a huge leap to move from one specific language to another, however technically challenging it might be. I believe that my interest in languages today – my need to explore not only English, but Italian and French in my writing – is because I find language difficult, not easy. And since I find it difficult, I also find it extremely interesting: a highly complex matter I need to keep studying, keep experimenting with in a continuous attempt to understand how it works.

*

I grew up in the monolingual communities of the Kibbutz movement. There was one approach to religion (atheism), one political belief and practice (socialism) and one language (Hebrew). There was no other belief system, no other tongue, and yet English was always in the far background – not a real language, but the possibility of language. Sure, it was not the language of the news, or of daily communication, or of books, and it was not related to any particular person or country, because I'd never been abroad. Instead, it was a language of two opposite realms: the first one was school, where I failed at English consistently and spectacularly. The second one belonged to the world of art and dream: it was the language I couldn't understand in films if I attempted to watch them without subtitles. And it was the language of music and movement: the words I couldn't follow when dancing to pop songs. In other words, it was a language deeply connected to visual and sonic images. It seems to me that without realising it, I had always associated English with the creative part of the mind. It was the language of Art.

It was also, for a brief episode, the language of escape. I have erased all memories of the Gulf War, when I was a teenager, except two. The first is the thick, sickening smell of the heavy gas mask on my face: the nauseating feel of the clinging plastic material around my eyes, the sense that I could not have it on my head for another split second because I couldn't breathe and was about to throw up. The second memory is of me and my cousin 'translating' Dire Straits' *Romeo and Juliet* on the phone in between air raid sirens, when we were allowed to take the masks off. Why did we choose to do this out of all things? It must have been an effective form of distraction from reality, because we had certainly never attempted to do anything like this before. I loved Dire Straits and she was good at English, so it must have seemed like a good idea.

My favourite Dire Straits' song was *Romeo and Juliet.* I had no idea what it was about but imagined it to be some kind of a deep philosophical contemplation on the nature of love. I was madly in love with the neighbour's son at the time, so it felt particularly urgent to learn a few insights from the song that might help me get his attention. My cousin's English was exceptional as far as I was concerned, so it was down to her to do the translation work while I listened attentively on the phone, waiting for the big revelations. I remember her translating lines like *You and me, babe, how about it?* Or *When we made love you used to cry* between one siren alarm and the next, and thinking: *Seriously? Seriously?? Is that – it?* I decided straight away that the practice of 'translation' was not that necessary after all, especially if I wished to enjoy the music. Better to imagine what the song was about – better to construct my own imagined meanings – than discovering the real ones.

Perhaps my expectation that the lyrics would add depth to the music also had to do with what I was used to when listening to many songs in Hebrew. In Israeli pop culture, it was not uncommon for a successful mainstream band to choose poetry for their lyrics. I assume it is still the case. After all, the word for song in Hebrew is the same word for Poem: שִׁיר (shiyr). The meaning of the word changes depending on the context, but it is still the same word, used as frequently in popular as in literary discourse.

*

There is a map of my childhood I've been trying to hold but it keeps disappearing: a personal geography where nothing stands still, especially words. Language is such a private thing: it carries pain in its syntax and grammar and sounds long after the physical or emotional pain has peaked. When I started writing poetry in English, the first thing I noticed was that my language became uncharacteristically clear. As a teenager, I wrote quite a few angry poems in Hebrew, most of them incomprehensible: a stream of consciousness with no real attempt to communicate. Years later, writing in English has forced me to clarify my thinking, because there was no stream of consciousness to work with. I couldn't pour down whatever I had in my mind on the page, because I had almost nothing in my mind when it came to English. This new way of writing has allowed me to try and construct images or ideas that were still communicative however complex, still aiming to reach a reader.

And yet, poetry is not only about the complexity of ideas and images. It is also strangely accessible. And this is another reason why I was drawn to poetry when I arrived in London with a deep sense of pain and a sudden urge to create, to do *something*: it was the only artform I could afford. As an aspiring writer, you don't need anything other than something to write with, and something to write on. Unlike most other artforms (theatre, film, music, visual arts) poetry writing does not require any special budget, instruments or materials, and unlike these artforms, it does not depend on other people (directors, performers) to bring it into life. Of course, poetry writing requires time – a lot of time – as well as an insane amount of stamina, but so do all other artforms. In other words, poetry, like language, is infinitely immediate. And it is this immediacy in a language I had already connected to the world of Art that has felt deeply and utterly stimulating from the moment I landed in the UK.

*

Language carries memories into the present, but on the night of 7 October 2023, memories rushed with such intensity – wave after wave of vivid childhood scenes – that I could no longer cope with words. I needed to find a physical object: something from my childhood that I could simply hold in my hands. I spent the entire night of 7 October sitting on the floor, holding on to an old photograph I managed to find only after hours of emptying every drawer and box.

The girl sitting next to me in the picture was my best friend, my first friend, and the only person I felt safe with during my early childhood years. I didn't acknowledge it to myself at the time. I just knew that I needed to be next to her all the time, and that as long as she was around, I would be fine. She was a confident, charismatic child. I was shy and fearful and a bit weird: I insisted on wearing winter clothes in the height of summer, and kept addressing my cat as 'he' long after he had ballooned up and gave birth to three kittens. But somehow, we connected. We didn't know, back then, that we would grow up to become artists in different countries and directions – she would pursue a career as a belly dancer; I, as a poet. But perhaps we already sensed this artistic rebellion within each other. We kept in touch until we were teenagers, long after I moved to another kibbutz. For years we would exchange letters – my handwriting chaotic, hers beautifully formed – and take long bus journeys to visit each other. Then, at some point, we lost contact completely and life continued to flow in separate directions.

For months I've been trying to write about the events that occurred on 7 October: on the way I found her phone number on a news website among a list of people who desperately needed help in finding their missing family members. Of the text I sent her, *Hi, it's Stav, your childhood friend*. Of the message I received from her after hours of waiting, when she wrote in Hebrew: *I've been looking for you on Facebook for years.* On her devastating update: *Mum is OK. Dad is missing.* I spent hours on social media that day, trying to find every tiny bit of information about what was happening in Be'eri, which meant I was also exposed to posts from fellow poets in the UK, celebrating and justifying the horrific scenes. I've been trying to write about the day which brought the most terrible news to my friend and so far, I haven't managed. I haven't managed to write a word. A complete failure of working in language.

If I try to mention specific people, I feel a horrible sense of guilt that I am taking advantage of their trauma, that I'm using their reality and grief, in order to get my own work published. I don't know how to talk about the death of people while making sure that what matters is their individuality, their life, not the way it ended. But I'm also aware that the way it ended is indeed relevant, and yet I don't know how to talk about that either. It is as if my mind, in an act of self-defence, is not willing to process the atrocities executed in Be'eri. At one point I decided to focus on the way I experienced the events in the UK during that day: the double horror of watching what happened in my childhood home while seeing the joyful reactions to it – the celebrations, the justifications. But this approach risked putting myself at the centre of it all, as if I had some kind of unique insight to offer, when all I could do is carry this enormous pain. Nothing works.

*

I have heard theories that a certain generation of children who grew up together in a kibbutz are more like siblings than friends because they spent their entire childhood together – not only days but nights too. I never really agreed with these theories which always felt simplistic to me, ignoring – as so often when it comes to social science – the complexity of individuals, of each child and their own entirely unique story. And I have long believed that if there was any lesson to be learned from the Kibbutz past experiment in radical socialism, it is that individuality always breaks through. Even if you take a group of children and raise them together from infancy under the same roof, values and beliefs, still they would turn out as beautifully and furiously different from one another as possible. And yet now, even though I haven't been in touch with my childhood friend for years, every time we speak, every time I hear her voice, I feel this deepest, warmest sensation, the one that tells me in no stronger terms: *you are home*. And despite everything that has happened, I hear her voice and immediately feel protected, as if I'm in the presence of someone who knows me most deeply, all the way from the earliest of childhood landscapes, the one in which words only begin to breathe and fall into form: you are home.

And also, you are home. By now, I have experienced major events in English: pregnancies, births, raising children, emergency stays in hospitals, moving cities, houses and jobs, and during all this time, the continuous attempts to study and write. Because I was never able to study in the UK, poetry writing has become more and more significant over the years: not only a form of creating but a way of studying: first the English language, and then everything else I could draw in. English is not a foreign language anymore. Instead, what remains of its foreignness is that it feels infinite: a matter that keeps expanding from one hour to the next. Not a single day passes without me having to check the meaning of one word or another in the dictionary. And because I keep learning new words, I experience English as a language that forces me to be alert, to constantly move between sound and meaning. Even during these most difficult months when I've kept having this painful, persistent realisation that *everything's changed,* English has remained an endless field that keeps expanding around me and taking me with it still the closest thing to living in a language in which I feel fully awake.

*

It's past midnight. Just as I thought I've finally completed working on my essay, I receive a message from my childhood friend. She sends me a picture another friend has just posted on his Facebook page. In the picture there are nine children sitting close together on a green and red wooden ladder in our nursery playground. In most of the pictures from my childhood, you can find me staring at the camera with no particular facial expression. But here, I'm smiling, even laughing. We're all laughing. The nursery teacher stands tall next to us, beaming with pride and the warmest of smiles. It is clearly a happy moment in the afternoon sun, and I suddenly miss them all so much. After all these months of mourning I'm still not able to process what happened in Be'eri. I don't know how to come to terms with the fact that the strong beautiful woman in the picture, our nursery teacher, was one of the many people killed on 7 October. One day I will have to find a way to say more, because carrying this deep sadness with no idea of how to express it has been very hard. Language is such a difficult matter, but I will have to keep wrestling with it, keep looking for words.

*

There are so many ways to leave a country. When I embarked on the plane to London, I left with the stubborn, youthful determination of never looking back. But it only now occurs to me that the process of leaving never ends. For months I've been running on the concrete pathways of Be'eri, again and again in my dreams. There is a map of my childhood in which I know all the directions: a lucid, intimate geography of longing and pain. In the dream it is always summer and I'm always running towards my childhood friend's home. Running towards my childhood. Maybe this is what I do. Running towards and from. When I left for the UK, I thought I could throw my first language away as if hurling a bag full of stones into the Mediterranean's furious waves. And yet, it turned out that I inadvertently carried quite a lot of it with me after all, because one of the few things I insisted on carrying with me on the plane was my guitar.

Here is the thing about my guitar. I've always found it quite difficult to sit still for a long time, which is a bit of an issue if you're aiming to write for a significant part of your day. My solution to this, in the last few years, has been to play the guitar while in the process of working on my poems. I'll start writing a poem, and as soon as I get stuck or a bit restless, I'll play the guitar (badly, it must be said) while reading and rereading the poem in progress, thinking how to move forward. By now it is impossible for me to write without reaching for the guitar at one point or another. It's one of the reasons I never work in libraries or cafes. But one thing that happens while I play, is that I often create or improvise fractions of songs. It is a rather unconscious process – the singing has neither quality nor depth, yet it is in Hebrew: a truly broken stream of consciousness.

Perhaps, after all, some kind of interaction between languages has always taken place when I work: one language that is almost too painful for me to hold outside of the unconscious, and another in which I can write with, in which I can play with words. Two languages that briefly touch and separate, like a circular activity initiated from some primary source or a single word that oscillates between two meanings, as if continuously moving between Song and Poem.

Poems

PIEDAD BONNETT*

Translated by Richard Gwyn

Prayer

For my days I ask of you, Lord
of the shipwrecks,
not water for my thirst, but thirst; not
dreams
but the desire for dreams. For
my nights,
all the darkness that is necessary to
drown my own darkness.

Scars

There is no scar, however brutal it might appear,
that does not enclose beauty.
It recounts a timely story,
tells something of pain. But also of its end.
Scars, then, are the stitches of
memory,
an imperfect conclusion that heals us, as
well as harming us. The form
that time finds to ensure
that we never forget our wounds.

On the Edge

What is terrible is the edge, not the abyss.
On the edge
there is an angel of light on the left side,
a long dark river on the right
and an uproar of trains as they leave the rails and
head into silence.
Everything
however much it trembles on the edge, is birth. And
only from the edge can the first light be seen the
brilliant white
that grows in our chest.
Never are we more human
than when the edge burns the naked soles of our feet.
Never are we more alone.
Never are we more orphaned.

Guard

I painted a dog to guard my door,
a dog sad and ferocious at the same time that
would deter any attacker.
But when I went to hang the dog on my door
I saw that there was no door, nor any windows.
I passed my hand over the rough wall looking for a crack,
maybe a hole. I understood that I was the wall,
and that without air, I was going to die,
that the only crack was inside of me and
that through the holes in my eyes a sad
dog looked out,
sad and ferocious at the same time.

* Piedad Bonnett is a Colombian poet who was awarded the Premio Reina Sofía for Latin American poetry in 2024. Five of the poems included here are taken from *Los Habitados* (2017), a collection that appeared following the suicide of Bonnett's son Daniel, a talented visual artist, in New York, in 2011. The poems also address the theme of possession by one's other – an enemy who torments its host. Daniel's life is the subject of Bonnett's memoir, *Lo que no tiene nombre* (That which has no name), 2013.

Kitchen

A kitchen might be the world,
a desert, a place for weeping.

There we were: two mothers talking very softly as
if there were children asleep in their rooms.

But there wasn't anyone. Only the echoes of silence
where once there had been music drilling through the walls.

We sought out words. We drank tea
gazing into the past's bitter well,

two mothers on the bridge that joins them their
hands grasping the void.

Guests

Tonight we have guests in the house
and they will stay over, sleep in your room. So I
dusted in all the corners,
I changed the sheets and plumped the pillow,
and put your old sweater away in a drawer, but first I
pressed my face against the wool, drowned in its
sweet bristling sea.
I won't tell them that the raven of your temples was sleepless here, nor
that a cheerless child bade farewell to you from the window.
I won't tell them that it's never daylight here.

I Ask the Pain to Persist

I ask the pain to persist.
Not to surrender to time, to embed
itself, like an eternal larva in my side
so that by its hand each day
you may be resurrected with your eyes intact, with
your light and your pain you may be resurrected
within me.
So that you don't die twice over
I ask that pain be my nourishment, that it
fan my flame, the blaze
to which you come each day to seek comfort from the cold landscapes of death.

Living between Languages

SUJATA BHATT

The first languages I learned to speak and was fluent in were Gujarati and Marathi. Gujarati was my native language, not only my mother's language but my father's language as well. Both sides of my family are Gujarati. When I was born, however, my parents lived in Pune, known as Poona in those days. Marathi was the language that was predominantly spoken in Poona, hence by the time I was three I was perfectly fluent in Gujarati and Marathi. I had picked up Marathi from the children in our neighbourhood and from my mother's Marathi friends. At that time, I heard and understood Hindi as well, but I stuck to speaking Gujarati and Marathi. Our Gujarati friends and relatives used to tease me for speaking so much Marathi.

My memories begin from the age of two-and-a-half to three, in fact I have many memories from the age of three. I can hear the sounds of Marathi and Gujarati in those memories.

I received my first major translation assignment when I was three. It may sound comical; however, certain events led to this unusual situation. First, my brother was born prematurely and needed to stay in an incubator. My mother, following doctor's orders, stayed in the hospital with my brother. No one in our extended family was able to come to help. This meant that my father had to take time off from work to look after me and to manage the household chores which included shopping for food at the various markets. Suddenly my father felt completely helpless because he could not speak Marathi. He knew Hindi of course and his native Gujarati and he had also studied Sanskrit. He was fluent in English. He was a physician and a virologist, working at the Virus Research Centre, as it was known then, which was founded by the Rockefeller Foundation. His bosses and many of the scientists he collaborated with were American. His colleagues came from all over India, his daily interactions with these colleagues and his publications were all in English. Until now not knowing Marathi had never been a problem for my father simply because my mother who was fluent in many more languages took care of all the shopping. My father knew that I spoke Marathi, and at that age of course I accompanied my mother everywhere. Therefore, my father decided that I would be his interpreter. My father would talk to me in Gujarati, telling me what to ask, what prices to negotiate and what to order from the shopkeepers. I would speak to them in Marathi and then in Gujarati tell my father what was discussed. My father naturally made all the decisions, and I was merely his faithful interpreter. I had a lot of fun. It was exciting to sit on my father's bicycle and to cruise around the city with him. It was unusual for my father to be with me and not at work for so long. It was sort of a holiday for me although I missed my mother. Sometimes we went to the hospital, which was more like a small clinic, and stood outside near the window of my mother's room. My father would call out to her, then she would come to the window and wave to us, and occasionally she would hold up my brother who was bundled up in warm clothes. My father did not want to take me inside the hospital, which was ultimately a place of infectious diseases. I did not know of course that my parents were extremely worried about my newborn brother's health.

At the time, being only three, I didn't realize how valuable my help was to my father, but it was something he never forgot. Over the years until the end of his life he would smile whenever he remembered those days and he would thank me again for helping him with my knowledge of Marathi.

Everything changed when I was five, my father received a research fellowship from Tulane University, and we arrived in New Orleans. I started to attend kindergarten and of course I had to learn English right away. The strange thing is that I have no memory of learning English. I do not remember the process of learning English. What I do remember is the feeling of culture shock. In the end, I did manage to learn English quickly, which is not surprising considering that I was only five. I have written a poem about this experience. It is entitled 'New Orleans Revisited' and can be found in my *Collected Poems*.

Soon Marathi started to fade away in my mind. Gujarati, however, remained. My mother continued to speak to us in Gujarati, which she did for the rest of her life even though she was perfectly fluent in English. My father spoke to us in both languages, Gujarati and English.

When I started school in New Orleans and began to learn the English alphabet, my mother taught me to read Gujarati and to write in Gujarati. She had prepared a special notebook filled with Gujarati exercises for me.

Nonetheless English was steadily becoming my native language. We stayed in New Orleans for several years, and when we returned to Poona it felt like another culture shock for my brother and me. New Orleans had started to feel like home. For my parents, on the other hand, returning to Poona was a true homecoming. Obviously, the English we had learned in New Orleans was a very distinct type of American English. The English we encountered in our schools in Poona was very different, it was a form of British Indian English. My father enrolled us in English medium schools in Poona since we already knew English. Furthermore, at that time in Poona the English medium schools were the better schools.

Now that we were back in India, we were reunited with the rest of our extended family, which led us to speak more Gujarati, especially with our cousins who hadn't learned any English yet. After a few more years in Poona we left again, this time permanently, for New Haven,

Connecticut, where my father accepted an invitation to join the faculty at the Yale School of Medicine.

My brother and I constantly adapted to each new situation, as children do, and after a few weeks in New Haven we spoke English with a clear Connecticut accent. Even though we spoke a lot of Gujarati at home with our parents, English had definitely become our native language.

When I was in my early twenties, I had written a long poem entitled 'Search for My Tongue' which explores my feeling of losing Gujarati even as I held on to it. I wrote the poem in English and Gujarati, always expressing the same things differently in each language. (This poem can also be found in my *Collected Poems*, and an excerpt from it in *PN Review* 100.)

I have noticed that I think in images and sounds, especially when I am deeply absorbed in writing, when everything simply flows, and the words seem to come from nowhere. Sometimes words come in multiple languages and sometimes there is an artistic reason for the text to be multilingual.

I live in Germany now. Although I learned German comparatively late in life, I still feel a strong emotional connection to the language, and I find that it provides some sense of home for my thoughts. At the same time, German is not 'my native language' in the sense that English is, and Gujarati used to be.

Our daughter grew up speaking both English and German. She is perfectly bilingual, fluent in both languages. Our grandchildren are also being raised to speak English and German. Our daughter speaks to them exclusively in English while our son-in-law speaks to them in German. Needless to say, it is fascinating to watch young children acquire language.

Verweile doch

ANTHONY RUDOLF

1. Aharon Appelfeld

In late 1996, Aharon Appelfeld and I travelled together to Lewes for the meeting commemorating the mother of our mutual friend Gabriel Josipovici. She, Sacha Rabinovitch (1910–1996), wrote and published poetry in English, her third or fourth language. She was also a translator of Clarice Lispector. Aharon Appelfeld, born in Czernowitz and one of the great Hebrew novelists of our or any age, wrote his books in his third or fourth language. On the train, I told him about or reminded him of my Parisian friend Piotr Rawicz, who was from L'viv, 200 miles south east of Czernowitz, passing through my ancestral town Ivano-Frankivsk.

Rawicz survived Auschwitz and later wrote his only novel, that masterpiece *Blood from the Sky*, in French, his fifth or was it sixth language. That's nothing, said Aharon, where he and I come from even the peasants speak six languages. Ah, I replied, but they don't write novels, even in their first language, let alone a masterpiece. Aharon conceded the point with his familiar world-weary smile. The previous time I had seen him was about a year earlier when he took me to lunch at Anna Ticho House, the loveliest museum in Jerusalem: chicken soup followed by apple strudel. Of course.

2. Joseph Rudolf

During his Austro-Hungarian army service at the end of the nineteenth century, my paternal grandfather, Joseph Rudolf, rose to the rank of sergeant in an Ulan, a cavalry regiment. His colonel was Herz Herzog alt Altbrecht von Wissenbach. Joseph lived in various places in East Galicia (now West Ukraine), before spending a year working in restaurants in Budapest and as a steward on a boat between the two capitals of the empire, Budapest and Vienna. The sergeant had earlier been a messenger boy between regiments because he spoke so many languages. His transport was a horse. He courted his younger cousin, Lilian Eilen, on horseback, near her shtetl of Zagorshchina. I finally met her in the mid 1980s in Danbury, Connecticut. The town is most famous for being the centre of the hat-making industry, or so George Steiner told me.

After what we can call his 'gap year' in Budapest, Joseph went home to his parents, Mechel Rudolf and Rosa Vogel Rudolf, but his ambition was to emigrate to London, where his older brother had already settled. He finally left, never to return, in either 1903 or 1905, having made the train journey to Hamburg docks, which involved a change at Auschwitz. His mother gave him a salami for the Hamburg-London boat. On arrival, he spent one night at the Jews Temporary Shelter in Mansell Street where his brother came to collect him next morning.

Joseph spoke at least nine languages – Yiddish, Hebrew, Ukrainian, Chochlis (dialect of Ukrainian), Polish, Romanian, Russian, Hungarian and English. Starting out as a trouser maker, he never left London, apart from periods during the Second Great War (as he called it), when he took his second-hand clothes and army surplus one-man-and-wife business, along with the youngest child Renee, to Luton and Cardiff; there were also occasional family holidays in Margate and Brighton. He died in 1980, at the age of ninety-nine or ninety-seven.

He spoke best his first and last languages. He never read a book apart from the Hebrew daily prayer-book, although he did read the Yiddish newspaper. That was it. While his colonel's name sounds like a character in a Viennese operetta, he himself always reminded me of minor characters in novels by a great writer of Austria-Hungary – up there with Kafka and Musil – Joseph Roth from Brody in West Ukraine. 'You should have become a doctor', Joseph said to me once, 'not sit all day alone at home translating books'.

3. Turgenev and Celan

> In days of doubt, in days of painful reflections on the various fates of my homeland, you alone are my support and mainstay, oh great, strong, true and free Russian tongue! How can one not fall into despair, seeing everything that is being done at home? But it is impossible to believe that such a language was not given to a great people!
>
> (from Turgenev's *Poems in Prose*, translated by Anthony Rudolf)

With the recent death of Pierre Joris, we have lost a major translator of Celan. Like Appelfeld, Paul Celan was from Czernowitz. One cannot discuss Celan's own poetry without entering into the terrain of translation, the poetics of the translational. I take the easy way out and leave you with two famous and heart-rending quotes from Goethe: 'Kennst du das Land, wo die Zitronen blühn?' and 'Verweile doch, du bist so schön'. ('Do you know the land where the lemon-trees blossom?' and 'Stay awhile, you are so beautiful'). The sentiments immediately remind me of my friend Gisèle Celan-Lestrange, the widow of Paul. I last met her at the funeral of Edmond Jabès in 1990. She died a few months later.

4. Russian Moments

One day, soon after we first met in the 1960s, Daniel Weissbort and I discovered we were both translating the work of the Soviet poet Yevgeny Vinokurov. We set about reading each other's many versions, mildly nervous about finding poems we had both translated. We discovered to our relief and astonishment that we had not translated a single poem in common, obviating the fear of comparison. What had happened was that we had tapped into different veins in the Russian poet's vast oeuvre. Daniel died in 2013 without our having had a discussion about organising a bigger book than our 1976 Carcanet volume, which was half his work, half mine.

I fear it cannot be a priority for me to edit a big collection of our new and revised translations, published and unpublished. Vinokurov was a very rare insider respected by the top émigré poets. By Anna Akhmatova too. I have just realised that this year is the centenary of his birth.

The first edition of *Doctor Zhivago* in English came out from Collins and Harvill Press in 1958, translated by Max Hayward and Manya Harari. My father bought this edition and I read it around 1959, before starting university Russian studies. The poetry translations at the end are poor. Donald Davie's marvellous *Poems of Doctor Zhivago*, translated and with a commentary, is now a forgotten book. Surely its original publisher, Manchester University Press, or Carcanet should reissue it.

There were two occasions and opportunities to use my vanishing spoken Russian: the first was in Ukraine in 1990–1 when I had an interpreter in Ivano-Frankivsk. Our only common language was Russian. In 1990 I was interviewed by Zinovy Zinik in the BBC Russian service on the subject of Octavio Paz and his recent Nobel Prize. I still read Russian literature, mostly in English or French. Recently I read the two volumes of Pasternak's prose (apart from *Doctor Zhivago*) edited by my Cambridge contemporary Christopher Barnes. Pasternak, for me, is the greatest Russian poet and writer of his generation.

Arctic Cities

SINÉAD MORRISSEY

For the Cossacks, Siberia was the future – either in pelts or timber –
as the Empire stepped East leaving tracks of bloody footprints
to the Vladivostok coast. Flung outpost of eaves and weatherboards,
dripping steadily from mid-April to unfathomable June,
here exile was largely character-building – with stoves, rye loaves,
foraging, the consolations of saxifrage and plug tobacco.
Summer, when it came, brief but extravagant, spiked the mind
like amphetamine. A child's voice calling through pines.

Stalin started a clock. To achieve the impossible – such as landing
two men on the moon – set a timeframe. Five years, exactly,
for *the electrification of the whole country.* The pistol crack.
From Rostov and Leningrad, Kaluga, Tver, in open-topped trains
that rolled for days past abandoned villages, revved-up youth decamped.
Teenagers built power stations. As if magicked out of permafrost,
fantastical cities sprang up along the 69th parallel – Magadan,
Igarka, Norilsk – where the Palace of Sport and the Palace of Culture

stared each other down across municipal squares
thousands of miles from anywhere. Forged by the disappeared,
whose bones packed out foundations, buildings rose high and straight
in cheery colour combinations – yellow and ochre, baby blue and pink –
doomed to blacken soon in soot from smoke-stacks
arranged around each town like satellites. Red Plenty underfoot:
in branching seams stuffed deep in the Earth's crust, gold, diamonds,
nickel, palladium, coal, sargassos of gas and oil

inspired Stakhanovite extraction quotas citizens in ushankas
and mittens fat as baseball catchers trudged in to meet.
Heating pipes grumbled, but obliged. There was snow and snow.
Cold and cold. Andromeda spun on its ever-narrowing axle,
a mistake in the firmament where the scissors slipped, poking out
too much. Girls left versions of themselves behind
as they walked to school – hoops you could pass your hand through,
where breath and winter and windlessness met.

Now, sure as frostbite, digit by digit, peripheral districts first,
cities atrophy. Bus-stops fly apart in storms or weather into crucifixes.
Inside derelict apartment blocks, a stiff Lady Dowager in baroque
headgear mounts each whitening staircase, encrusting with her touch.
Clocks grow tentacles. Come early spring – unfolding earlier
year on year – sinkholes offer lessons in spectacular collapse
as ice-roads turn impassible. There is rain and rain. Slush and slush.
Car graveyards. Anthrax. Hydrofluorocarbon stars.

Caprice

ANGELA LEIGHTON

I was four or five when my Italian godmother gave me a book with the rather formal dedication: 'Ad Angela, perchè non sdimentichi il nostro italiano' (so you won't forget our Italian language) – that 'nostro' drawing me into an early belonging as warm as it was inclusive. We were about to return to Britain, as we did at the end of every summer since my birth, and Zia Mimmina wanted me to remember my mother- (and mother's) tongue. The book was *Pinocchio*, the story of the wooden puppet whose nose was as long as the lies he told. Looking at it again sets me wondering about language, particularly our so-called first, native or mother-language – but also about lies. Robert Creeley once reported how someone asked, at the end of a poetry reading: 'Is that a real poem, or did you just make it up?' Between reality and making it up, there's always language, our passport and go-between, our shared contract and occasion for personal invention. A 'real poem' comes, as any writer knows, from the most complex work of making it up.

It may have been that same summer in Naples when I asked the classic childhood question: 'Mamma, where did I come from?' There was a moment's pause, then a brief answer as she hung out the washing on our balcony: 'from Mummy's tummy'. Was it the belittling brevity of the answer, its unlikely matter-of-factness, or the insultingly silly rhyme of the English that drew a furious response from me? 'Non è vero', I accused, slipping, as our family always did, into Italian for extra volume and emotional effect. 'Ok. So where did you come from?' she replied, keeping her cool. Without a moment's hesitation I retorted, now tearfully angry and still louder in Italian: 'It's not true. I was found under the motorway bridge, where the ships are and the chimneys, on the road past the port to the seaside.' Delivered with a gabbling conviction, I wonder now what bizarre quarrel I was playing out, with her, myself, my different languages. What fantasy of origins was I making up in that very precise, unpremeditated location? In a split-second I had claimed as my own a rough, anonymous, industrial shadowland on the city's outskirts – yet a place that was real enough, and that I can still pinpoint today on the Naples bypass. Was I, in that moment of impulsive self-assertion, also saving something of 'il nostro italiano' against the encroachments of English, already becoming my main language? 'Ma non fare capricci', Mamma interrupted, finally raising her voice and using a word that, in Italian, nicely links the caprices of the imagination with childish tears and tantrums.

Reading Michael Schmidt's intriguing editorial in *PNR* 281 alongside Gabriel Josipovici's 'Is There Such a Thing as a Native Language?' I find myself, like them, puzzling over the languages we learn, then half-forget, half-remember. Which was the first, the original one? 'Something, I Forget' (the title of my own latest volume of poems) might be a phrase for that lifelong forgetting which leaves all sorts of archaeological deposits in the burial grounds of memory. Certainly, as English came to dominate my childhood tongue, Italian went a little underground – perhaps under that motorway bridge which I'd desperately tried to claim as my peculiar birthright.

One of the problems of talking about 'a native language' is in fact the singular noun, which seems to offer a quick passport to nationality or identity (also too often assumed to be in the singular). Maybe if we could learn to think in the plural, of languages and identities, origins and legacies, we might come closer to the changing richness of who we are. After all, not only are we layered by languages learned throughout life, but words in any language are themselves layered by changing histories and meanings: there's an evening in *serenade*, a ghost in *larva*, a spirit in a *sprightly* gait, spilt milk in a *galaxy*, star-scapes in *considering*. What is native, natal, innate or natural is already on the move in the languages we use. And birth is hardly the beginning, either. Who knows what tunes we first hear in the womb, or what music our speech recalls from far back in a shared, primordial life? Language, as any writer knows, often *makes* the sense we only think it conveys, just as it gave the child in me that happy coincidence of finding, after all, that I might be just another Neapolitan street urchin (*scugnizzo*). Certainly, such improvised self-invention seemed to come from nothing more than a caprice of language, a self recognised in the act of saying it. (Or was it just one of Pinocchio's lies?)

'Non fare capricci'. Deep in the Italian history of that word one hears, incorrectly, a capering goat, but also, in a truer etymological line, 'un capo riccio', a head of spines. For *un riccio* could be a sea urchin (*riccio di mare*) or a hedgehog, each spiked like a shock or surprise. Perhaps it's not only in poetry that we discover, and try to revive, those constantly shifting, half-forgotten, half-remembered movements of the language – or rather, of various languages, as their histories, musics, trades connect them. So, 'fare capricci' (whether inspired fantasies or childish tantrums) might be a good place to start.

Five Poems

MARIA BANUȘ (1914–1999)

Translated by John Gallas

March Wind

There's a mad March wind in the turn of the world:
Today it has taken its turn with me.
I believe in the apples, round and ripe,
That will figure its pause and pregnancy.

The whole earth shakes. It shakes with life.
The March wind tumbles the turning sky.
We believe in the drive of newmade thoughts,
The startled *now,* and the scoured *I.*

The March wind howls in the turning world:
Believe in your strength. The trees are bare.
Invisible turbulence beats the branches.
Infinite darkness fills the air.

So we mend...

So we mend, sublime and slow, like pines,
Tending to our hurts ourselves. And through
Fresh veins the branching, salving sap succeeds.
At each old wound the ambered resin bleeds.

A scar is sweet: it coddles like a nest,
And in it life revives, and hums anew:
While in each swarming branch the flux revives
The matrix of our bright, insistent lives.

Remember the fire

Remember the fire. The hurt. The Spring.
The blizzard of flame that came to stay?
It had made us one: it had torn us in two:
And its turbulent heat had led us astray.

And then, when that first, sharp blaze of life
Refused to relinquish our hearts so long,
When we carried the burden of still seeming young,
There were different dreams that kept us strong.

And if, today, we are one and the same
And hold to each other though time storms by,
Perhaps it is peace by another name:

That we looked for the fire, though the fire was done;
For the words that bring the world to light:
The innocent passengers of the sun.

Bucharest after rain

This is the moment, this is the hour, maybe,
When all my old, accustomed cells just died,
(Each seven years it happens, so they say)
And the new were born, and took their toddling way
Under the sunwet chestnut trees with me.

This is the infant, newskinned afternoon:
Pinkish and soft, with patches of watered frost.
The silken tarmac plays in the lightened breeze
Under its wondering nave of sparkled trees.
Whether I earned it or earned it not – it is June.

Perhaps I bought it with long, moth-eaten years:
My scribbling, gibbetish thoughts and ashy smile.
But how can you earn or pay for this? To find
This bright flamingo hour; this newmade mind?
This trumpeting of chestnut trees; these tears.

April

The tune of ages takes its way.
I feel it now, and wait for more.
You hold me through the passing years,
Each passion kinder than before.

The startling cymbals of our youth
Are now no longer yours or mine.
The same old powers of strength and joy
Come wisely with our older wine.

Ours the many-coloured Autumn.
Ours the land of reddled trees.
Ours the sombre cellar and the pungent glass...

How can I know what unquiet breeze,
What April, what wild prince might pass:
And break the Attic calm with thunder in the grass.

The Long Crossing

JANE DURAN

I grew up hearing Spanish spoken by my parents' friends, many of whom were, like my father, exiles from the Spanish Civil War, but who enjoyed a complicity and understanding as the freedom and pleasure of speaking, relaxing into, their own language burst from them whenever they gathered in a room. My father would play Spanish folk songs on the piano so everyone could sing. A Spanish accent permeated everyone's English. My father could not say '*Spain*', but *es-Spain*; Spanish doesn't have the English soft 'g or j' sound so he would say *yust* instead of *just*; the soft, round 'h' in the word '*home*' was more guttural, harsher; and those rolled *r's* of course. To me, the mother-tongue accent is a positive affirmation of identity and brings another dimension and musicality into English. It says '*I'm from there*'.

The intonations of Spanish were part of my life from the very beginning, but at home when I was a child we spoke English. My mother was American, she was a great reader, and passed on her passionate knowledge and love of poetry to me. One of the ways she learned Spanish was by avidly reading Spanish literature: she avoided looking up every unfamiliar word but learned new words by their context. My father was a linguist, he knew several languages and his English was excellent. He was rigorous about syntax and fascinated with word derivations. If I made the mistake of asking him the meaning of a word when I was in the middle of doing my homework, he would embark on a long explanation of its etymology.

When my father was posted by the UN to a regional commission in Santiago, we all moved to Chile. Suddenly everyone around me was speaking Spanish – called *Castellano* in Chile, or Castilian. The inflections of Chilean Spanish are gently persuasive, fast and singsong. The refuge of language: it affords a kind of protection – or none at all if you don't speak it. It comes freighted with countless associations and connotations which cling to it. Understanding and speaking the language of a country where you live offers safety and community and a road ahead. I was already eleven when I was immersed in this new culture, too late to become bilingual. No matter how fluent I became, I would still be a *gringa* in Chile.

The other day I took my guitar from its case after many years of not playing. My right hand had forgotten the finger-picking and strums for the American and Latin American songs I used to play. I had to slowly retrieve the patterns, string by string, very laborious. But after a few days the pace quickened and my fingers began to remember. It's a bit like that for me with Spanish. When I have been back in Spain for a week or so the words start to come easily again, I begin to think in Spanish, I retrieve words long unused, I eagerly scoop up and learn new words and idioms. But my accent is more Chilean than Spanish, and if I'm tired I sometimes can't pronounce the double *rr* as in the word *arrollo* or *barrio*. My origins become evident in different ways, just as my use of English and my accent and manner set me apart as American in England, though I have lived here for most of my life.

When I visit Spain I revel in the language and in what feels like another me: the way I interact with people changes and is closely connected with language. And I feel, when I am in Spain among my father's family, my Spanish cousins and my old friends, that it is where I am also somehow deeply connected to and belong. Yet there is always something of longing, somewhere missed. What I see in the landscape will not be what someone living there sees: I'm very aware that my presence is fleeting, that I want to take everything in and that I am being torn away. A similar awareness of familiarity and loss happens to me when I visit America, and this finds its way I think into the language of my poems.

Translation is another borderland where two languages meet and dialogue, but what is the power balance between the original and the translated text? When I began to co-translate Lorca's *Gypsy Ballads* with Gloria García Lorca, who is bilingual, what did we hope to carry through into English? The *Gypsy Ballads* are lyrical, dreamlike, unresolved narratives, suggested or evoked through powerful imagery that is rooted in the traditions and landscape of Lorca's Andalucía. If we tried to replicate the form and assonance patterns in English, we would certainly sacrifice Lorca's meanings. If we tried to unpack (for clarity), or alter or embellish an image, we would lose its unique particularity, force and resonance, and perhaps its interaction with imagery across the sequence. From the outset we decided that we would go for fidelity to the meanings, fidelity to the particularity of Lorca's images.

This also meant that in some cases we decided to keep a number of words in the original Spanish (defined later in our Notes) if no word existed in English that conveyed the same or similar meaning, ambiguity or resonances. For instance in the poem 'Mockery of Don Pedro on Horseback', the Spanish word *laguna* means both a pond, lagoon and also a gap, lacuna, both meanings important in the poem. The adjective *aljamiado* in the poem 'San Rafael' describes Spanish written in Arabic characters: central to the poem is the fusion of Arabic and Christian cultures in Córdoba. Lorca's 1935 lecture on the *Gypsy Ballads* calls San Rafael a 'peregrine archangel who lives in the Bible and the Koran, perhaps a better friend of Muslims than of Christians, and who fishes in the river of Córdoba'.[1] There is no single equivalent word for *aljamiado* in English.

In translating each ballad there are inevitable losses and failures. But as we worked there were moments when the original poem began to inhabit our translation; you could see through the English to the Spanish text:

> Far below the river sings:
> a ruffle of sky and leaves.
> The new light is crowned
> with pumpkin flowers.
> Oh sorrow of the gypsies!
> Clean sorrow, always alone.
> Oh sorrow of secret riverbed
> and remote daybreak!
>
> 'Ballad of the Black Sorrow'

Walter Benjamin wrote: 'It is the task of the translator to release in his own language that pure language which is under the spell of another, to liberate the language imprisoned in a work in his re-creation of that work'. In the same essay he quotes from Rudolf Pannwitz: 'The basic error of the translator is that he preserves the state in which his own language happens to be instead of allowing his language to be powerfully affected by the foreign tongue... He must expand and deepen his language by means of the foreign language'.[2]

I love the idea of the seismic presence of the original language in the translated poem. How can this be achieved? It is immensely helpful to have a knowledge of the language and cultural context of the work to be translated, and to work with someone who is bilingual, as I did, so that the resonances, the nuances of words and feeling, the full spirit of the original poem can make the long crossing.

1 Translation by Christopher Maurer, *Gypsy Ballads*, Enitharmon Press, 2011, p. 201.

2 'The Task of the Translator', from *Illuminations* by Walter Benjamin, translated by Harry Zorn, Pimlico, 1999, pp. 80–81.

Who Remembers

MARILYN HACKER

Who remembers Léonor de Montaigne,
an unloved only child, merely a daughter?
Her (unloved) mother, women servants, taught her
manners and household matters, to be clean,
how to cook and, one would hope, to garden.
A governess, perhaps. No Latin tutor.
No fencing, equitation. No world tour.
The essay on educating (well-born) men
her father wrote stipulated all these.
And who remembers Jacqueline Pascal,
whose father taught her everything her brother
learned. Church writings only – poetry's
too worldly. Though she could word a miracle.
Marie, uncloistered, always remembered her

Marie, uncloistered, always remembered her
months in the convent, when to fast, pray,
and meditate, alone, brought her such joy
she almost starved. A Mother Superior
or priest opined that the exterior
life might be her designated way,
with Latin, French, a graduate degree,
at twenty-four, and just after the war.
Then, steerage class to France, within her means,
the battlefield detritus that she sorted,
the chapels, river, and the coup de foudre.
Then, seven children, living on rice and beans,
twenty-odd F train stops into Queens –
a life whose sense was purposeful disorder.

How prayerful, sometimes, total disorder
seems. I have dismembered my life
and am on my knees in the wind, in the half-
dark, on prickly grasses, on the border
between summer and fall. I hear discord, or
is it only the wind, that seems to laugh
at everything? I took a photograph
of the street, and one of the front doors. Dir-
ection unknown, toward the square, the road away?
Metaphoric knees, but real confusion.
I think of talking about it with Marie,
have to remind myself again she's gone.
The hills are there, implacable blue sky.
The street is there, and leading out of town.

The street is there, and leading out of town,
– or in, a heatwaved Tuesday, driving back
from the vast supermarket in Gignac
laden with yoghurt, paper towels, brown
eggs, in the fire of early afternoon.
The square's like the aftermath of an attack –
that man sprawled on a bench could be in shock.
I remember a poem by Josephine Jacobsen
where hell is a Mexico City parking lot
past noon, and there's no place left in the shade.
A stray dog's stretched out under the arcade,
sand-coloured, vaguely wolfish no-named-breed.
Entropy spreads like oil. The concrete's hot.
The man, the dog, are breathing. They're not dead.

The man, the dog, are breathing. They aren't dead.
Just stoned unconscious by the canicule.
Somewhere a waterfall, a mountain pool,
a path shaded by conifers, that led
into a clearing, still breezy, ahead
of midday heat, the estival misrule
of what's misheard, mistranslated. A minuscule
vowel shift can shift everything: your bed-
mate, your next meal, what your window looks
out on in first morning, reflects it back
for you to contemplate, thinking of books
you've read, or haven't read, or stopped reading.
Whose are the words that I don't know I'm needing,
as the page after the last page goes black?

The page after the last page shifts to black,
then back to white, another empty screen
a probable, imaginary scene
projected there – an embrace, an attack
or an omission. Get over your knack
for melodrama! The dog's got his own
home, he's at the window, its wrought-iron
balcony, beside 'his person', the attrac-
tive crop-haired ceramicist, who has a shop
downstairs, opposite the grocery's
side wall, where the road to LeBarry
begins. Down at the base, the hiking trail
to the abandoned castle starts. I stop
there, turn back, breathing hard up the hill.

I turned back, breathing hard, went up the hill
to my afternoon attic of books,
notebooks, 'devices', distractions, in the nooks
of the couch, 'en ligne', out on the terrace, fill-
ing the freezer. Then the heatwave fell,
like migraine, a lead curtain, like rebukes
from a friend when friendship ends. J. smokes
in the armchair, where, earlier, in still-
cool morning, I drank coffee. All shutters drawn
against the sun. Upstairs, the ceiling fan
hums, the only noise. Claim peace, regain
cloistered silence, that's not a rented room
no one else enters. That's the hoped-for rain,
(an essay by Léonor de Montaigne...)

My Father Was Born in Florina

EVAN JONES

My father was born in Florina, Greece, just after the Second World War and during the Civil War. My grandfather fought on the Albanian front and I heard something about one of his brothers killed in the fighting that came after. In 1950, my grandparents, my father and his older brother left Northern Greece for the safety of a country that hasn't fought a war on its shores since 1812. Young enough that he didn't attend school in Greece, my father never learned to read and write in Greek – let alone the second language his father's family spoke – Macedonian. After the First World War and the events of the *Μεγάλη καταστροφή* (the 'Great Catastrophe' – the population exchange following the Greco-Turkish War), my mother's grandmother travelled with her sister from a village near Tripoli, in the Peloponnese, through Ellis Island to New York. When her sister died, she went west to Denver, then back east to Chicago, where she married my great-grandfather (also from a village near Tripoli). They left Chicago then moved to Montreal – my grandfather was born there – went back to Chicago, and finally settled in Toronto, where they had two more sons. My mother was raised by her grandmother and learned Greek in the kitchen of a small house on Berkeley Street through which every relative from the Tripoli area seemed to pass. Though the nearby church offered Greek lessons, my mother never learned to read and write in Greek.

There are contradictory stories about my language learning. The first is that my mother spoke only Greek to me so I'd grow up bilingual. One day, watching me call *'Ελα, παιδιά!'*, to children outside, she realised this wouldn't work. The second is that, by the age of one, and with the aid of *Sesame Street*, I could recite the alphabet. Neither of these sounds right and together they make no sense, but they were repeated enough times that they stuck. Whatever the truth of these family myths, I had the sounds of Greek and English in my head from childhood. Greek was spoken in our home, my parents sharing it as a secret language – Christmas presents, money issues, arguments were covered in such a way that my sisters and I had no idea what was happening. Outside the house, it was the language we were scolded in. We learned from older cousins to swear up a storm, and impressively – I was told by Bulgarians who, decades later, asked what words I knew in Macedonian.

In my twenties, I began to study Modern Greek. By thirty, I could read and write, though my vocabulary has slipped so much. Funny that it's vocabulary that goes, not necessarily grammar or construction. I published my first book of poetry in Canada and it included, at its centre, translations of a Greek poet not at all well known outside of Greece. I talked when I could about surrealism and read Cavafy, Seferis, Elytis and Ritsos. I moved to Thessaloniki and stayed first with an aunt and then in student accommodations. I met a young man who after a coffee and conversation, said, You look Greek but you don't act Greek. But I knew that already. I was the one inside calling, Come here!, to everyone outside.

Prayer

DOAA KADDAH

Doaa, my name, means prayer in Arabic – just prayer. It is a very Islamic name. It is not the female version of Mohammed, for that would be first-degree close affinity to the prophet, like Fatma or Khadiga. But I would say it is the female version of Hussein, Ali – second or third degree, yet still discriminably Islamic to the Arabic or Muslim ear.

To Muslims, my name is a bullhorn. To everyone else, it's just a name with two guttural sounds absent from the Latin alphabet. It's a neon sign flashing across my forehead.

These were the exact words I told an Australian man in my regular coffee shop in Berlin, where I currently reside, two days ago when he asked me about my name as I was preparing to write this piece.

'Are you from a different ethnic group in Egypt? Are you Coptic? I never heard this name before in Egypt,' he asked.

'No, Tony, my name is very Islamic. I was born during the 4 a.m. call to prayer: Du'aa el Fajr. But then my family decided to call me Donna.'

They never called me Doaa; it was just for official purposes. Why always baffled me, which might explain why I ended up as a cultural anthropologist critical of taken-for-granted societal assumptions people keep passing down to others as *Mosalamat*, an Arabic word for givens.

Mosalamat, the noun, comes from tasleem, the verb – to pass from one hand to another. To deliver without an explanation, to pass it along and assume that you will fit into it, forever trying to accommodate it instead of bending to fit my mould.

I could have stayed with Donna, the name my family called me, though my birth certificate says otherwise. I had to reclaim the name as an adult in college so that my head would be cleared from the potential noise of incessant questions that still haunt me, no matter how much I try to escape.

I was born and raised in Egypt by my single mother, together with my two siblings. She is a very Sufi Muslim, inward with the tenets of Sufism. She never talked about it to us, and I know she performed her Sufi-inspired prayers and sing-alongs, but never in front of me. Maybe with her circle, and I was never invited to participate. Because I am not a Sufi, for her, it was not a decision I made, and she never forced any of her beliefs on me. I realized how deeply Sufi my mother was when I accompanied her on a trip to Jerusalem and met her friends. I was a true anthropologist, indeed, watching mystic-inspired performances at times and visiting familiar holy Islamic sites at others.

With my father, on the other hand, I sang along to Islamic songs during my childhood and learned how to conduct proper Duaa – practicing what my name preaches. When I hang up the phone with him on Facetime in Berlin, he says, 'La elah ela Allah', no god but Allah, and then I say, 'Mohamed Rasul Allah', Mohamed is his prophet. Islamic gestures with my father signify our special bond. An absent father but a present Muslim, always available to reciprocate how we say goodbye to each other. When I will no longer be able to tell him 'Mohamed Rasul Allah' as we end our phone call, when he is no longer on the other end of the line – this is already a moment I dread.

But my mother was from a different school – not a fan of the visible portals of religion or any public display of affection as a marker of difference. I finally understood what she was trying to do after years. 'Donna, 99 percent of our religion is how you deal with people and only one percent is reserved to the rules. Heaven is not reserved to Muslims only. We are not special. It is for everyone. We are just one way and not the only way.'

When I was twelve, my mother took me out of national schools and enrolled me in an American school. That's where I met my first American: Mrs. Mary, my music teacher. She taught me how to play the flute and sing along to 'One Moment in Time'. I still remember how fast she spoke, her English racing like a scene from one of those Disney movies my grandfather used to bring back from his yearly trips to the States. Why is Mrs. Mary speaking so fast? Do Americans ever catch their breath?

I can still hear her asking, 'What's your name?' My name is Donna. But in that moment, I realised I had to keep up – with their breakneck pace, their clipped words, the way they seemed to chew through sentences. Where are the rest of the letters, Mrs. Mary? Is this how other Arabic speakers feel about the Egyptian tongue? It felt oddly familiar – how something proper and whole transforms into quick slang, dialects and accents, leaving you wondering what got lost along the way.

By tenth grade, I was known as Donna, and this duality between Donna and Doaa was normalised and never challenged. English was also my predominant language. This identity shift became all the more pronounced when, at one moment, my English teacher, Mr. Oliver, forced me to confront one *Mosalamat* of our household: my dual names.

First, it was an essay about my family's cats. A harmless topic, yet my work was riddled with grammatical and spelling errors and all the imprints of what it means to learn English as a non-native speaker. Mr. Oliver copied my essay for the class. For forty-five minutes, the students tore it apart word by word. Laughter echoed as my errors became the object of their ridicule, my work the emblem of what it meant to fail at translation.

The second moment came when Mr. Oliver asked me directly, 'Why do you call yourself Donna? Do you identify with a Western name?' I answered as best I could. 'That's what my family called me', I said. 'Right,' he responded with barely disguised judgment. 'I'm sure they did.'

Ever since this comment, my classmates noticed this duality. Some of them didn't know about the very Islamic Doaa. 'So you are not Donna? Wait, why would you do that? It is like if you are called Nabawya (a very Egyptian name with rural connotation), and you want people to call you Sandra (a Western white name)? Why?'

Teenagers can also be cruel. I felt the need to defend myself against things I had no part in – a need to defend my 'nativity' to Donna, a strange name untethered to our familial genealogy.

This duality between Donna and Doaa – a name chosen and a name used – was never just a personal dilemma. It mirrored the contradictions of the world I grew up in. Maadi, the neighbourhood where I was raised, sits squarely at the intersection of histories and shifting identities. Once a space reserved for British colonialists, Egyptian royalty, intelligentsia and European families (as Gabriel Josipovici aptly describes it in *A Life*), Maadi transformed after Egypt's 1952 post-colonial ruptures. The upheaval saw longtime residents of Maadi leave permanently and new families such as mine moving in. For example, Jewish families with deep ties to Egypt and my hometown like Josipovici's, European passport holders – all began to leave or were forced to leave. The streets they used to walk, the neighbourhoods they once called home, no longer belonged to them. Mosseri Avenue, for example, became El-Nahda Street – where I was born and raised. Renamed and reimagined, it was a Pan-Arabist attempt to create something new while burying what came before.

But the past doesn't disappear just because you change a sign. Maadi became a palimpsest, layered with new street names, people and identities. People like my family, whose story felt just as patched together as those streets. There was my grandfather, a once-exiled Yemeni politician, wrapped in the migrations and struggles of Yemen's past and its turbulent present. Then my grandmother, incredibly pale with Turkish origins, whose unfamiliarity set her apart even within our family. On my father's rural side, the whispers were harder to pin down, carrying rumors of Jewish lineage – that we were part of a well-known Jewish family 'back in the day'. It was always vague, unspoken, shrouded in the kind of mystery people learn not to question. Just like those renamed streets, our family's identity seemed eternally caught in a cycle of erasure and reinvention, constantly adapting to fit the moment without thoroughly understanding the past to shake it off.

I come from a historically Western town; I have a contemporary Western name, and I am not either of those things. My native language, Egyptian Arabic, is spoken at home at times, but my mother speaks English, and with friends, a weird hybrid of Egyptian Arabic and English is still practiced to this day by some Maadists and Egyptians. Formal Arabic is treated as a complementary language you don't need to learn. Taken once a week, it felt irrelevant to my lived experience and day-to-day interactions.

My body's natural inclinations were at odds with proper conduct. It had to be disciplined to align with sensibilities I was expected to adopt but did not inherently belong to. Gesturing with hands while speaking was frowned upon – such behaviour was associated with the lower class. We were not farmers, *falaheen*, like my father's family, nor Bedouins, as in my grandfather's Yemeni ancestry. We were refined, embodying a performative ideal shaped by enlightened sensibilities: their language, their habits, their self-disciplined nature. Our so-called 'backward' origins had to evolve to meet these higher standards. The body had to be tamed, and any connection to nature severed.

Manicures had to be pristine, free of scratches, or I risked being perceived as a domestic worker. When seated, legs had to remain closed; I was, after all, a lady and had to appear poised. Words had to be chosen carefully, delicately, for directness was vulgar. This refinement had to be evident in every aspect – from the elegance of our attire to the fluidity with which we spoke Western languages. We were striving to embody the enlightened ideals of European sensibilities. Our language was all designed to tame and elevate us from our so-called primitive origins to the modern standard.

But then, there was German – its structure, its logic, its unapologetic complexity. Unlike the delicate English and Egyptian I was taught to wield, German felt raw yet meticulously exacting, offering a space of clarity I had never known. Its sharp angles and precise grammar became a refuge, a stark contrast to the performative grace I was expected to embody. Speaking German was not about refinement or taming; it was about precision, and honesty. Here, I did not need to dance around words or fold myself into a posture of elegance.

During my twenties, I started travelling in the summer to Germany, learning the language and meeting a new culture, which made me feel like quite an attractive person. A feeling I never got, being a tall 180cm woman in Egypt, where macho patriarchal males were much shorter than me. German – and the Germans – were refreshingly clear. Words meant exactly what they meant. So did the people. Cutting to the chase, direct. What a sweet relief from the subtext I had to read in English and Egyptian Arabic and being lost in translations. The price I had to pay was just very hard grammar, a verb that sometimes stayed at the end, new pronunciations like *isch*, and learning how to roll my tongue on that one. And again, extremely fast-speaking people. The position of one word forever changed the form, pronunciation and grammar of the next. With dialects as confusing as the diverse Arabic tongue, I learned the basics of High German, *Hochdeutsch*, and for my first MA found myself in the south, in Ingolstadt and Munich, with their strong Bavarian dialects. I guess this is their 'Egyptian', huh?

I now live in Berlin, where it almost feels like everyone is estranged in some way. Along with the luggage we brought from our home countries, there's a familiar estrangement from whatever ailed us to leave in the first place. I feel at home in my strangeness, inhabiting the spaces between languages, where the locals can never fully grasp who I really am. Fractured, fragmented, incongruent – never able to be stitched together, no matter how many words are used to fill the cracks. You could speak English, German, and Arabic, but nobody really cares, as long as you're understood and leave them alone when necessary.

In Berlin, I finally understood my relationship with my languages – a place where I could finally unpack my personal and ancestral luggage. I discovered that each language I speak holds its own emotive memory. English is my working language, the academic language. The anthropologist in me resides there. It is the language I learned the most through schooling, the one where academic concepts and jargon sometimes lack direct translation into Egyptian Arabic. It embodies the thinking self, the mind-centered epistemologies that required my body to stay still, an empty vessel, as English penetrated every sphere of my existence. It is also the language I must prove mastery over, the yardstick by which the refinement and cultivation of a third-world citizen are measured. I have evolved, and English is the proof.

Meanwhile, Egyptian Arabic feels informal compared to the 'native' formal Arabic tongue. It is the only language I don't feel the need to dress up in to inhabit – it is my home wear. It is closer to my body, forgiving when I slip in English words or mix and match phrases to translate myself for others or even for myself. It carries the Egyptian songs of the eighties and nineties, my dance moves, my bodily gestures and expressions. It's the playlist I turn to when Berlin's cold – both metaphorical and literal – becomes too much for my Egyptian sensibilities.

Egyptian Arabic still holds my anger tightly, waiting for me to signal any need for temporary relief. It works wonders against creepy drunk men late at night in Berlin. I lean into the entrenched stereotype of the volatile, unpredictable Arab and their protective pack, ready to defend their 'woman'. The moment they hear the sounds of letters unavailable in the Latin alphabet, they pause, recalibrating their actions. Arabic also holds my grief. It is the language I yelled in during protests in Germany for a Free Egypt in 2011 and for a Free Palestine in 2024. The former was celebrated and legal; the latter is now illegal, as Arabic is banned from German protests. They might need to understand what these 'natives' are spewing.

But is Arabic really my native language? Native implies that my words could always translate the worlds I find myself in. Native suggests a language that can fully grip me, encompass me. My native language and my 'native' failed to make sense to me, and I felt compelled to make sense of them. Unsurprisingly, this led me to pursue a PhD on my hometown, Maadi, where I sought to understand why I felt so estranged while growing up in this environment. I questioned whether there were objective conditions that could explain the subjective feeling of alienation I experienced in such an artificial setting.

As I was deep in the research process, I found myself listening to Gabriel Josipovici's 2011 audio recording of his experiences in Maadi, left at the American University in Cairo by a historian who wrote a book on Maadi. I was captivated by this man. I listened to this audio while cleaning, running errands and organizing my weekly meals. Here was someone who had lived in Maadi, who articulated the very things I had failed to put into words.

Gabriel noticed the same dualities I had – the divide between the European quarters and the so-called 'native Arab' spaces. He spoke critically yet thoughtfully about the artificiality of Maadi, even mentioning the nearby Arabic village. His reflections were a revelation, echoing my own yearnings and my inability to make this place feel like home truly. He was the only 'Maadist' who consistently brought up the world outside Maadi, a world he felt cut off from. Who was this man? I Googled him, and wow – he was a big deal! How had I not known about him? Should I reach out? What if my impulsivity got me into trouble? My experiences during fieldwork had made me wary of approaching strangers.

Wait – he was the author of a book I had read back in 2010. That book had validated my doubts about the arrogance of positivist epistemologies when I was studying educational psychology. *What Ever Happened to Modernism?* I needed to talk to this person who had once affirmed my fears about the hubris of histories. Despite hailing from a different discipline, his work reflected similar yearnings and preoccupations.

Gabriel smoothed out for me the unease of approaching potential interlocuters for my research. His response was humble and swift, and our Zoom meeting became a catalyst for a beautiful unfolding. I couldn't have asked for a smoother interaction. From our very first meeting, he put me at ease so entirely that the roles felt reversed – I became the interviewee, and he barely needed to be interviewed. I think I ended up talking far more than he did! What followed were numerous emails and the arrival of two much-needed books for my PhD, sent to my address in Berlin. One of them was a book of his – *A Life*. This thoughtful gesture deeply moved me.

In my reply, I tried to express my gratitude by weaving together the three languages I speak. I wrote:

> And finally, I just received your beautiful gift… I am sorry, but I have to thank you again! Vielen Dank in German, Shoukran gedan in Arabic, and thank you for this. I took a picture of the envelope. The most dreadful part of the day now, the long Berlin commutes, are the most enjoyable, thanks to you.
>
> Also, thank you so much for sharing your thoughts with me, but as usual, I would have never figured this out by myself. I think this is why meeting you beautifully complicated and messed up a very straightforward and clean-cut narrative I thought I had in mind about Maadi, about the 'colonial encounter.' I also see the pitfalls of narrating history from above and how all these individual nuances and experiences get lost to make a complete picture whole when it can never be such, I guess, which prompts me to question the analytical and writing choices I must make.

My words felt empty and insincere. I tried expressing my gratitude in every language I knew – Egyptian Arabic with 'shokran awi' (thanks a lot), German with 'danke', and English with 'thank you'. Yet none of it felt adequate when addressing a renowned literary novelist, a vital voice in contemporary British literature, who has built a career through the power of words. And here I was, fumbling with language, blurting out, 'Shokran gedan!'

But as our friendship grew, so did my comfort in expressing myself. Over time, I found new ways to communicate – through gestures and body language that transcended words, even if they clashed with the reserved norms of Egyptian bourgeois sensibilities.

> I wrote to Gabriel again:
>
> I am already reading *A Life*, and I must say I missed a couple of stops so far because of how much I traversed elsewhere. I hope to come across the story you mentioned; maybe I will.
>
> I also found myself savoring every word, and I felt a bit selfish. I do not doubt that so many Egyptians would love to hear your story and listen to you. So many Maadi enthusiasts would be thrilled to hear you narrate your fascinating journey beyond academic circles. If I ever make it to London, it would be a great chance for it.
>
> P.S. I noticed your beautiful words and handwriting on the front page today (Doaa, from one quasi Maadian to another – and with all good wishes for the happy completion of your thesis) I am filled with awe as I place my hand on my head and say: on my head, *ala rasi*.

Gabriel responded the next day, curious about my expression:

> Tell me about the hand on the head?
> Gabriel

I replied, diving into the cultural significance of the gesture:

> Thank you for asking about the expression. I had to delve deeper into a gesture I wouldn't have consciously questioned but habitually performed.
>
> When someone wants to demonstrate a tremendous amount of respect and recognition for someone, they lay their palm on the top of their head. They lay it on top and say, 'Ala rasi.' Some might make a slight tap as well. Egyptians who are more

connected to their rural upbringing and/or from more humble and modest origins would place both palms on the sides of their head, as shown in the attached picture.

Would an Egyptian do that with their tarboosh before? It may be so, but I don't know. I also see that it is a traditional Bedouin Arab gesture. I attached another, making it a bit corny. Forgive me.

It implies the highest respect and recognition for someone because it is on the head. Unlike its antithesis, of course, which is 'Ala regly,' meaning 'on my leg,' or 'Ala gazmety,' meaning 'on my shoes.' It is the lowest form of recognition and has no respectful connotation whatsoever.

It might explain why an Iraqi journalist found no possible words to capture his feelings and instead expressed a strong 'ala gazmty' gesture, flying and attacking former President Bush. The journalist threw BOTH his shoes at him, as shown in the video below.

'Ala rasi' can also be an appropriate response in other contexts. Arabs mostly use it to say 'you are welcome' after someone has thanked them. It might also be when someone asks them where they are from, and they say 'Ala rasi' to show similar high regard for their hometown. For example, my experiences with the Syrian community have been chiefly colored by the high regard they have for Egyptians because they felt Egyptians treated them with grace after the Syrian civil war. So when I say I am from Egypt, they say, 'The Egyptians, 3ala rasna,' and then explain why.

> So, you are always 'Ala rasi,' adding 'wallahi' for emphasis.

Best,
Doaa

On another occasion, I found myself expressing yet again a bodily gesture that came so habitually to me. Gabriel sent the following photo with the subject line 'Greetings from Lewes'.

I replied: 'Brilliant photo! I love it! Waving my hand back first, then placing my hand next to my heart, tapping twice, and saying, "Much love to you."'

After my email exchanges with Gabriel – how I use my body to say 'Much love to you', or even 'thank you' – I began to realize that these gestures were uncovering a mode of being within me that I hadn't known existed. It was a way of expressing myself that stood in stark contrast to the constraints of my elite upbringing. Gabriel's openness and lack of judgment created a space where I could explore this part of myself, unearthing it and freeing it from the limitations I had long internalized.

It also led me to wonder whether my complex relationship with the languages I speak is an exception or a rule. Would I feel the same if I were fluent in formal Arabic – the way I habitually speak, dance, and spark conversations in Egyptian Arabic? What if I hadn't grown up in Maadi? Would my connection to language and identity have shifted if English had been my first language, instead of one I awkwardly adopted as a twelve-year-old with a slight moustache and rounded shoulders, struggling to keep up with Americans and their intrusive questions about who I was? And what about German – my escape? A language of rigid social and grammatical rules that taught me to tone down my loudness, to fit in, to be taken seriously.

Maybe if I had been encouraged to embody these languages as distinct modes of being, I wouldn't have felt so constrained and conflicted. Perhaps the cracks between my languages would have been filled. Maybe if I had felt accepted as I am, without the pressure or imposition to inhabit myself as Doaa or as Donna in Maadi, then maybe I would have felt 'enough' for Egyptian Arabic, for English, for German. But no matter what I did, I was never enough – neither for the academic halls and daily life in Germany, nor for the English-speaking circles and streets of Cairo.

I shared these thoughts with Gabriel during a Zoom call, and he reminded me that others have felt the same. He spoke of Kafka, whose father pressured him to abandon his Jewish identity and assimilate into German culture, believing it to be superior. Parents often want the best for their children, but this can mean surrendering to the hegemonic order of the world – a legacy of the European Enlightenment that demands everyone orbit around its ideals.

Perhaps my native language didn't fail me; perhaps it was the other way around. Or perhaps language itself is insufficient – a construct severed from the body, from manual labour, from the so-called 'primitive' peoples that modernity sought to evolve beyond. My familial trajectory seems to echo this. Maybe bodily gestures, like language, are learned and not truly native. Yet, with Gabriel, I found myself using my hands in ways I rarely had before. He tapped into a clogged reservoir I hadn't realized existed within me.

Encountering Gabriel was profoundly therapeutic. Through his work and presence, he offered an invitation to balance, a recognition of the paradoxes of the human condition, and, most importantly, the grace to let go.

And yet, I am still left wondering: how native am I, and how native is my language, really?

Two Poems

KATHERINE HORREX

The Loomhouses

Because of this almost scurvifying lack of light. No matter
if the phrase embodies the wrong vitamin. Just give me wall-length panes
and an earthen floor. "Light-bearing interfaces." Windows will be called this down
the line. A light-expanding whitewashed interior. Four rush bottom chairs
and a bobbin wheel. Filaments plucked, like vermicelli from the vats,
ten neighbourhoods in length. Loom as air-zither. With a pail for tipping under the frame
for humidity's sake. And then a crock of oaten cakes. A stack of creels. Give
me my foot-a-bouncing on the treadle. Give me the worms. The way they move
one segment at a time. The gnarled and puffed-up rhizomes.
Shucked out with boiling. Galoons. Gros de Naples. This scarf. Such brocade
denies the worm its mothdom. Never to put out horns beyond the cloth.

An empress drinks tea beneath a mulberry tree and into her cup will plop
a single fibrous eider-coloured bundle. She'll know instinctively to use
the fished-out threads, the life I plump for now in spite of the hike to Red Bank
with the wallet and back. For I'll take this over any factory. Cloth-in-the-ears;
the many looms a-clatter at once. Stammering brickwork and hole-punch
confetti; striped dresses from the offcuts. This house is a loom
threaded with exquisite days and nights! But if you wake me I'll show
to live on Silk Street is to tuck slantwise between Argos
and Aldi. Grey as a reservoir below hills, these roads trail off toward the Hilton.
The weaver's cottages nought but nubs and all knocked down.
I wish light would come at a greater decibel! Not the way the buses
bring it, in episodic side-street form, in sheets.

Netherlands

sit on my hands and spend no money
since buying tickets to the wrong museum.

Serious thoughts about the piecemeal
movement of the windmills to Zaandam.

Beautiful thatched octagonal smocks
winched over the railway catenary

somewhere in the poldered North.
Not one more lavish breakfast now. One fat spliff...

no wish to not waste tickets
could lead me to the CGI Van Gogh!

Brassy weather pouring down the Herrengracht
mid-week. Overfresh, the chill from Oosterdok.

But it was never this frigid scene. How
to match the intricacy of the Grachtenpanden:

nine square panes in their demurely angled frames.
The timber lintel and the stucco corbel scrolls.

The neck, the bell, the step, the spout...
GableWatch would marvel at such ways

to meet the infinite upward! I cannot call it
sky again. In a red window a woman tilts her hips.

Furnace in the glass by night.
A partnership of fourteen years drains off.

The streets, crossed by unfamiliar ways,
are magical once more.

Quirky as a crayon-scape. Sails set
in majestic crowns twirling over the reeds at Het

Twiske. Baskets of sheer Dutchness
limed and limed again for us.

Two Pieces

FABIO MORÁBITO

Translated by Richard Gwyn

The Other Language

I remember when I didn't yet speak two languages. My mother tongue spoke through me; it took me by the hand and I let myself be guided by it, without question. A bit like breathing. Nobody devotes their time to breathing; air stimulates the lungs and other respiratory tracts while we focus on other things. Likewise, the mother tongue does all the work while we just get on with living. Rather than speaking, we breathe by means of words, we inhale language, which is barely speaking at all. Of course I knew that other languages existed, even at school they taught me another language, but it's one thing to learn foreign words and phrases in a classroom and quite another to be speaking another language, which implies some kind of inner transformation. Learning a second language puts one's own into context, it turns the mother tongue into a language, impermanent, like all languages that have ever existed. Translation takes this contextualisation to an extreme. It immerses the mother tongue in the great linguistic broth of the world and delivers yet another blow to our illusions of fixity, rootedness and eternity. Every time we translate a foreign text into our mother tongue, it is impossible not to take the journey – at least to some degree – in the opposite direction; that is, to weigh up the appropriateness of the sentence or paragraph we have just translated, mentally 'retranslating' it to check its accuracy within the source text, and it is at this point of 'suitability testing' that we become more conscious of the uniqueness and the limitations of our own language. Perhaps this is why some people feel an aversion towards translation. From the perspective of the language we have learned, our mother tongue is no longer the same, and we articulate that also, we 'de-mother' it, because life, in a sense, is a long, often painful process of de-mothering, of converting our mother tongues (our parents, the people we fell in love with, the places of our childhood, as well as our most traumatic experiences and deep-rooted fears) into other languages. It is an endless work of secularisation and detachment, and dying, which is the ultimate detachment, is also the act of opening oneself definitively to all languages. That is why we die with our lips open. This opening, disturbing for many, is not produced by the last exhalation of the body but by the desire to say, to finally speak with the whole mouth, and perhaps what ultimately kills us is that first syllable we exhale in a language that encompasses all the others and possesses all articulated sounds, an opulence for which no one is prepared and which makes us absolute polyglots just at the moment we become mute forever.

A Room of One's Own

At a time of uncertainty in my life I decided to apply myself to translation. My vocation for study was at a standstill, and this was coupled with a seemingly trivial fact: for the first time I had a room of my own. I had just dropped out of an unrewarding university course and although I knew what I wanted to do, I didn't know how to achieve it or, rather, how to begin. It was then that translation came to the rescue. I needed to immerse myself in a credible task. Without telling anyone, and in a clandestine manner, I began to translate poetry from my mother tongue, translating it into the learned language that had adopted me, as it were, definitively. That, in the first place, was anomalous: translating from the mother tongue into an acquired language, when the vast majority of translators do the opposite. But the task didn't frighten me, because I finally had a room of my own. In addition, I had a girlfriend who loved me very much, among other things because of my accent, which she considered delightful. I confided my new life plan only to her and I immediately noticed her concern. With the clairvoyance unique to lovers, she saw in translation an enemy. Perhaps she feared that by immersing myself in the adopted language I would lose my foreign accent. As for me, I realised that translating poems from my mother tongue was a way of saying goodbye to it, without necessarily getting closer to the adopted language, so I felt like a foreigner twice over, lost between two languages, a bilingual being without a home. My girlfriend intuited all of this and kissed me passionately. She kissed my accent, inhaled it from my mouth because she sensed that, once extinguished, my love for her would also be extinguished, as indeed happened. She was my true foreign language, which I managed to make my own thanks to translation. Once I knew how to translate (it took me a couple of years, shut away in my own room), we broke up. I have confused memories of that time, one of the most crucial in my life, when my foreign accent, love and a room of my own were painfully intertwined.

Ur-Language

HOWARD COOPER

1.
My paternal grandfather, Ya'akov Faibishiak – born in 1892 in Brzeziny, Poland, twenty kilometres east of Łódź – was an illiterate Yiddish-speaking tailor in a town long noted for its Jewish tailors. Yet if to be 'illiterate' means to be unable to read or write, I am making an assumption about him: literacy was highly prized amongst even the most impoverished of eastern European Jewry in the nineteenth century and he would have been fluent in Polish and Yiddish (as well as prayerbook Hebrew) even before he arrived in Scotland around 1910 and began to assimilate Glaswegian English into his polyglot sensibility. But reading was something else.

My father, born in 1917, recalled reading Yiddish newspapers as an adolescent to his father Ya'akov – by then known as Jack (the Biblical name Ya'akov is traditionally translated as Jacob). Why would he have been reading to his father? Perhaps my grandfather's eyesight was failing? Or was it the inability to read the language he grew up with? My father, Archie – he changed his name in adult life from his birth name Haskel, a Yiddishised derivative of the Biblical Yehezkel ('Ezekiel') – never explained what was surely more than a bonding exercise in the tenements of the Gorbals. He was a man filled with silences (and secrets), and when he let slip this rare, touching glimpse into his early life, I was too shy to inquire any further. But that my father knew how to read Yiddish was a revelation to me. For I had never heard him speak Yiddish; and although a smattering of leftover Yiddish words and phrases might be casually dropped into the conversations of postwar British Jews – people were often *meshuggah*; families could be filled with *broigus*, particularly if the men were dating (or God forbid marrying) *shikses* (cf. Philip Roth) – Yiddish was representative of a world gratefully left behind: there was little nostalgia for *der heim* and even less for an unmourned past of poverty and persecution.

Geographically, *der heim* was that vast hinterland, stretching from Lithuania, Latvia and Estonia to Ukraine, Poland, Romania and Russia – the 'Bloodlands' in Timothy Snyder's chilling phrase – where Yiddish had been the *lingua franca*. Yet the assimilationist project of Jewish immigrants, at the end of the nineteenth century and beginning of the twentieth, led to Yiddish's virtual disappearance – at least as a living presence and richly textured worldview – within a generation and a half of Jews' arrival into this country and concomitant integration into British Jewry. 'Cooper' had replaced Faibishiak before my father was born – the *echt*-native surname was derived, so family mythology had it, from Glasgow's leading grocery chain Cooper & Co.

Yet perhaps I am too quick to dismiss the emotional dynamic contained in my father's reading to his father. My grandfather spent long hours, six days a week, labouring in a tailoring factory: time with a Yiddish newspaper may have been a rare opportunity for a shared activity whilst an epochal transformation was underway. For – although this may be a not untypical immigrant experience – the intellectual distance travelled within a generation seems astonishing. My father's engagement with, and love of, language – of literacy if not of speech – was an alchemical mixture of his own temperament interacting with an eldest-born's opportunity for a grammar school education. There was six years of Latin, four of Greek, and an immersion in English language literature, part of the evidence for which was a profusely underlined and battered *Collected Works* of Shakespeare in our family home that I recall thumbing through in my teenage years with an awed sense of the hidden learning within this taciturn man.

And he was as familiar with Robbie Burns as he was with classical Hebrew – he knew the poetry of both by heart, along with the Romantics, and could read from the unpunctuated Torah scroll in the synagogue with a minimum of preparation. Thirty years after leaving school he was still more capable with Latin than I ever became: I always struggled with the language, needing his help with my homework, and translating my A-level set texts of Ovid's *Metamorphoses* and Caesar's *Gallic Wars* came as naturally to him as if he was still at Hutchesons' Grammar.

I have not inherited his proficiency with languages – I don't have the ear. That polyglot sensibility of my illiterate grandfather and literate father feels like it belongs to a lost era. What I have perhaps inherited – and made my own – is an enjoyment of, and a limited capacity to use, my birth language, English; and an appreciation of the cultural resource of Biblical Hebrew – the Ur-language behind all languages, as the mythopoeic fantasy of Judaic culture conceives it to be.

2.
Ur – 'primeval, primitive, primordial, proto-' – is traced by etymologists to Middle High German, from where it migrated into English texts in the nineteenth century. Be that as it may, to the Biblical ear it resonates with the original home, Ur, of the original ancestor of the Hebrew people, Abraham (Genesis 11:28,31). This is neither etymology nor even folk etymology – it is merely the kind of imaginative association that the traditional rabbinic playfulness with language promotes. For the Talmudic rabbis of old, the Hebrew Bible was treated as a sacred repository of words available to be read, heard and interpreted in multiple ways. The sacred texts, composed in a sacred language, might often be prescriptive, were sometimes proscriptive, but were always suggestive. The genre of exegetical literature the rabbis developed – known as 'midrash', from the Hebrew root 'to seek', 'to inquire' – was a 'seeking out' of meanings beyond a literal understanding of the words. Texts could never be

reduced to a single meaning because within the mythology of the emerging Judaic consciousness of the post-Biblical era, each verse, each word, each letter of the canonical corpus expressed a divine essence – a divine, godly wisdom – that could never be exhausted.

Because the Hebrew language itself was viewed as partaking of divinity – and because the original texts were composed without punctuation, thereby allowing for a variety of readings for each word – the rabbinic imagination could release, as it were, innate meanings incarnated within Biblical words, phrases and sentences.

An example: there is a verse in the Book of Isaiah, chapter 54, verse 13, that reads, in its plain meaning: 'All your children – *banayich* – shall be taught about the Divine, and great shall be the peace of your children'. Centuries later, a rabbinic conversation in the Talmud suggests that the text is to be read – i.e. understood – as containing an undisclosed meaning: 'Do not read "*banayich*", "your children"', it says, 'but *bonayich*, "your builders"'. The rabbis here are not interested in what the text means 'literally', as we moderns might put it, but what it suggests, what it implies, what further truth it illuminates, what additional message it generates. The original text's consonants allow for, are available for, a different vocalisation, and this different vocalisation creates a different noun – which then offers a larger, two-fold vision.

Firstly, this rabbinic re-reading is promoting a social and cultural agenda: that each generation's children are the 'builders' of Jewish life; and that the future wellbeing of the Jewish community depended on the education of the children of the community. This notion became a staple for Judaic culture for the next two millennia: thus my grandfather may have lacked opportunities for literacy, but he ensured that his son did not.

We can note that this time-worn Talmudic reading of the Isaiah text, the imaginative amplification of a meaning inherent in the text but awaiting its explicators, its so-called 'interpreters', takes the text *out of its context* and offers a homiletical/metaphorical reading that the rabbis believed was implicit within the original sacred script. Texts were, in essence, polymorphic in their intent, for they were filled with a divine energy that was polymorphic in its essence. Language itself, as we shall see later, was a manifestation of divinity.

But secondly, this rabbinic re-reading of the original, this creative mis-reading of the original, allows the text to be understood in a new way *within its context*, at the level of the sentence itself in relation to the sentences around it. For in this passage, the author of the text – whom the text names as 'Isaiah', although we do not know who composed the text – is anticipating for an exiled community the imminent restoration and re-building of the city of Jerusalem following its destruction by the Babylonians (in 587 B.C.). The original author of the text may already be writing in the knowledge of the restoration – projecting backwards, as it were – but whatever the circumstances in which the original text is created, more than half a millennium later, rabbinic explicators of the text generate a reading that speaks of the prophet Isaiah's hopefulness for the future and the prophet's belief that Jerusalem will be built again with the help of 'builders' imbued with the spirit of the Divine.

Yet such a reading, by midrashists of the second to sixth century A.D., is historically determined. The Talmud was composed by rabbis living in a further historical exile, after the destruction for a second time of their beloved Jerusalem, in 70 A.D. By imbuing the original text with a future-oriented hopefulness focused on 'builders' who are themselves imbued with the spirit of the Divine, they are implicitly suggesting to those who are again living in exile that they should allow themselves to remain hopeful for a future return to, and rebuilding of, Zion.

The plasticity of Biblical Hebrew language, of sacred consonants that await the addition of, the articulation of, vowels in order to render up multiple readings, was integrated into an underlying rabbinic approach to the community's sacred texts: the rabbis viewed the sacred corpus of the literature they had inherited as a vast textual web of divine self-disclosure revealing the interconnectedness of all reality. Everything was connected to everything else through the medium of language. A word or phrase in one part of the canon was read in the light of the same word or phrase in another Biblical book – a form of intertextuality that was possible because language itself was sacred and had a single source. Divinity shone through individual texts, it was believed, but also through the juxtaposition of texts which could spark new readings, new meanings, that were latent, awaiting their expositors. The art of interpretation became, for the rabbis, a sacred activity.

3.

Over time, the rabbis of the Talmud and midrash found ways of justifying their belief, their basic premise, their supreme fiction, that the language of the Hebrew Bible – independent of its meaning/s – was sacred, holy. They used a verse from the Psalms – 'By the word (*bidvar*) of God were the heavens made' (33:6) – to point towards the power of the Hebrew alphabet itself to be generative of the world in which they lived.

Of course the notion of a divine Creator is inscribed at the very start of the Biblical narrative (Genesis 1:1): 'In the beginning God created the heavens and the earth' (AV translation); 'When God began to create heaven and earth...' (Robert Alter and others; all translations are, as we know, interpretations). But the later rabbinic explicators of the text went beyond the notion of a creator God to articulate a more radical view, namely that the medium of creation was language itself: viz. 'by the *word* of God...'.

It helps that Hebrew prefixes can carry a range of meanings. Here, the initial letter *b* of *bidvar* can be translated as 'by, in, with, or through' – so the idea of creation *with*, by means of, *words* is implicit in the original text. But the more radical world-view lies dormant within the text until its time is ripe to emerge.

Yet such a reading – one that became foundational for a more mystically-inclined approach to Jewish literature, theology and practice – does not emerge *ex nihilo*, as it were. The Genesis text itself is already alert – be it consciously or unconsciously – to the power of language within creation. For in that famous opening paragraph of the Hebrew Bible, the narrators plant at the heart of creation (initiated by a divine Creator) the idea that the medium for creation is language: thus 'And God *said*, "Let there be light", and there was light' (1:3).

In other words, within the Biblical myth, the narrators portray primordial formlessness being filled with a specific form of creative activity: at each stage of creation they describe, imagine, a God who uses *language* to generate each new act of creation. 'And God said... and God said... and God said...' is the refrain. It echoes through the opening chapter of Genesis. God 'speaks' the universe into being, as it were. Here the Hebraic storytellers conceive of a Conceiver/Creator who – *mirabile dictu* – is a mirror image of themselves: language-welding creators of worlds. Why wouldn't they project their own giftedness with words onto and into their own portrait of the divine Author of the world? They knew the power of language to create worlds.

From the idea that God uses language to create the world – heavens and earth and everything within them, including us – there emerges the idea that language itself is sacred. Not just the words of scripture are sacred – for they reveal the divine – but the twenty-two letters of the Hebrew alphabet are sacred in themselves. For they are the building blocks of creation, of everything that ever was and is and will be. God's toolkit, so to speak, is Hebrew, 'articulated' in endless permutations.

This mythopoeic fantasy receives its earliest full incarnation in a short cosmological work of systematic but speculative thought, the *Sefer Yetzirah*, the 'Book of Creation'. Written in Palestine at some stage between the second and sixth centuries A.D., the unknown author sets aside the dominant tradition and culture of Biblical exegesis, of midrash, and develops a quasi-'scientific' theosophy in which the laws of the universe are linguistic. Using a simile with which we are now familiar, God is portrayed as a builder, a craftsman who uses the twenty-two letters of the Hebrew alphabet as the material of creation: 'God drew them, hewed them, combined them, weighed them, interchanged them, and through them produced the whole creation and everything that is destined to come into being'.

There are thirty-two mysterious pathways and ten emanations of divine power (*sefirot*) – but all must use, and are vehicles for, the letters of the alphabet: 'By means of the twenty two letters, by giving them a form and shape, by mixing them and combining them in different ways, God made the soul of all that which has been created and all of that which will be'.

This esoteric, enigmatic treatise does not draw upon Hebrew Biblical texts and traditional rabbinic exegetical methods, but it existed alongside more mainstream thought for a thousand years, available for those who were attracted to such speculative metaphysics. This changed in 1570 when Rabbi Isaac Luria left Egypt and arrived in Safed, a small Galilean town renowned as a centre for Kabbalistic learning. He brought with him, and developed there, a new mythology in which the primordial power of the Hebrew language and alphabet was a central motif.

For Luria, every moment of existence is sustained through the vibrational power of language, and the human use of language is one of the ways in which divinity is made present in the world. The spiritual struggle of humanity for transformation depended, for Luria, on paying precise attention to how language manifested and investing it with intentionality when articulated – particularly in the everyday poetry that Jews call 'prayer'. He wrote down little of his teachings but his mystical theosophy, disseminated by his followers, penetrated mainstream Jewish theology and had particular appeal for those who sought out a more personal and existential mode of practice.

4.

I have been tracing in this essay the grandiose perspective of an ethno-cultural self-absorption in which classical Hebrew is the Ur-language beneath all languages. While being secular at heart I can still enjoy the mythopoeic fantasy of this *Weltanschauung*. It informs my thinking about the transformative potential of language, well-used. We share linguistic worlds with those who preceded us, and I like to think I hear the echoes and reverberations of that archaic mythos in the poetry my father knew by heart, but never shared with me:

... a sense sublime
Of something far more deeply interfused...
A motion and a spirit, that impels
All thinking things, all objects of all thought,
And rolls through all things.

Hyacinths

PADRAIG REGAN

A meditation at a symposium on queer Irish poetry: 25 January 2025

They have been roughly stuffed
into a glass jug
whose tapering throat

is not quite wide enough
to accommodate
their collective girth,

so their cut ends float
halfway down the water,

white & indecent
as a razor clam
exposing the full nude length
of its edible self.

Specimens. Long thumbs.
Entirely subjected.

Stripped of the privacy
the soil afforded
to the pale foundations

(nothing that colourless
was meant to be seen, surely)
the blooms drew themselves up from;

the blooms being only
an attempt at distraction,
saying:

Look here! Look up here!
Look at how we've arrived
at the perfect midpoint

between blue and purple,
& constellated there!
Our hundred eyelids!

O my membranous darlings,
don't you know that beauty
will be convulsive
or it will not be at all.

*

Can I stand by that 'only'?
Aren't they also

an opening, a gas-flame
gesture to the grand machine
of reproduction,

essentially genital?
& therefore symbol

for all we've joyously

renounced, or otherwise
othered. All this talk
of kinship & trauma

has me flitting back
to the feverish
post-surgical days

last winter, when my lover
was a pin-cushion,
all deep-rent fissure

no chemical could soothe,
& his uterus
was burning somewhere

having been evicted
from the self it never quite
had a home inside.

*

No-one quoted Ovid:
If, in a garden, someone steps on the stem
of a violet or rigid poppy,
or breaks a lily's gold-shuddering tongues,
its head droops downwards, withered & submissive,
& can't be righted, but gazes at the earth:
so it was with the dying boy, his neck
abdicating the cargo of his head.
To do so would be only obvious.

*

Glutted with water,
swollen & softened
from the constant pump-work
of their unstoppered veins,

or perhaps it is the curved
surface of the glass
making them bulge like that,
a trick of the light's

variable piercing
– fast glass & slow water –
ergo further proof
it is in the lens

& not the thing itself
where meaning resides
& nothing is immune
to the warp of optics.

But lately, things
have been rearing up,
bald & factual.
Chief among them: death

& chiefly my father's,
which is no less real
for having happened
only in the future.

*

According to Burke,
colour is beautiful
when it is *soft* & *mild*

& if not *soft* & *mild*,
at least *diversified*
or *mixed in such a manner, and with such gradations,*
that it is impossible to fix the bounds.

He'd love you, hyacinths,
not just your warmed-up blues
but the unhurried,

onionish gradient
from green to white that falls
along your foot-long necks.

*

But the beauty of flowers
is boring, isn't it?

So obvious, & so
indulgently divorced
from the background slaughter
that scores our living,

it seems almost an act
of wilful ignorance
to go on staring

at these small, compound
instances of genes
flourishing outwards.

They need a Mapplethorpe
or an O'Keefe

to warm their cool tissues,
& light their carnivals
of pure architecture

until their self-involved
silences bend under
the yolk of sympathy.

*

(Or do I mean the beauty of men?)

*

Burke on proportion:
Now, if it be allowed that very different and even contrary forms and dispositions are consistent with beauty, it amounts I believe to a concession, that no certain measures, operating from a natural principle, are necessary to produce it.

*

My father on the tumour:
It doesn't hurt exactly, but I can feel it in there.

& for months afterwards,
every time my lover
put his fingers inside me,

all I could think about
was that four-inch, wormish
nodulated clod

of feral cells stressing
its emphatic presence
in my father's colon,

& I would picture it
a kind of translucent,
bloodless, spectral white:

an anti-colour
I could attach to no
real object in the world

until the hyacinths
paraded their absent
bulbs in that glass jug.

*

(Didn't Burke also say:
the colours of beautiful bodies must not be dusky or
muddy, but clean and fair?
& isn't that enough

for us to discredit
whatever else he might
say about the matter?)

*

For so long the only
language I could find
to mirror my desires

was a hall of mirrors:
Narcissus → Dorian → the vampire's erasure:

wholly inadequate
    to the circumstance
    of loving someone

who, through sheer force of will
& hormone & stitching,

    has brought their body
closer to the blueprint
    mine can't escape from.

*

    While sketching, Hopkins
would arrange his own limbs
    in imitation of
    the thing observed

so he could better feel
    the disposition
of its unique selving.

    What posture could I
adopt to get across
the hyacinths – inhabit

    their upwards pouring
& culmination in
both pistil & stamen?

*

I took one home with me.
On the bus from Dublin,
it held its protest well

against the heat seeping
    from all the sleeping
& unsleeping bodies.

    I covered it up
in a ceramic pot,

    it fit like an eel
in the oesophagus

of an antique sailor,

    or a rattlesnake
poking its dry lure out
    from a drainage pipe.

For three days it has stood there
on a shelf in the bedroom.

Its green parts see by eating,
or eat by seeing:
    a long eye watching

as each of us took turns
at being root & bloom
    sequentially,

    reciprocally
straddling each other
& drawing force upwards

from each other's bodies,
& there at the apex
    I wasn't thinking

    is this hyacinth?
    Is this? I was just
commensurate with *hyacinth:*

    simply being all
    vertical flightpath
& pointilist fanfare,

achieving some vegetal
    relief from thinking.

*

        (Days later,
    I would lift it out
& see its stalk gone black,

cauterised with mould,
as though it was vision
that it subsisted on.)

In Search of My Silenced Language

PARWANA FAYYAZ

As an Afghan growing up speaking Persian/Dari, I read Maulana Rumi. I encountered his poetry at school and heard his verses recited both at home and in gatherings, large and small. His words echoed from the tongue of my illiterate Grandmother Lion, sometimes fragmented, sometimes whole, always alive on her moving lips. Rumi was everywhere – his lines adorned letterheads and featured in every television programme even remotely connected to the sweet language of the Parsi speakers. One of his most famous lines serves as the perfect introduction to his renowned work, *Masnavi Ma'navi*:

بشنو از نی چون حکایت می‌کند
از جدایی‌ها شکایت می‌کند
کز نِیستان تا مرا بُبریده‌اند
در نفیرم مرد و زن نالیده‌اند

> Listen to the reed as it tells its tale,
> complaining of separations from within.
> As soon as they separate me from my reed-earth
> in my chest, men and women have screamed therein.
> (my own translation)

I could never grasp what this poem meant, why it was expressed the way it was, or how it was said – like this. I must have been about fifteen at the time. I could not even begin to comprehend the sense of the reed and the earth, the voice resonating within it, or the breath that gave it life – let alone come close to the depth of meaning that would prove so much more intellectually captivating at the age of twenty-one. This is when I encountered the poem in a broken English translation by Coleman Barks –

> Listen to the story told by the reed, of being separated,
> since I was cut from the reedbed, I have made this prime sound.

When I read Rumi's poem in English translation and found myself coming remarkably close to its meaning, I asked myself: What had happened there?

At the age of nineteen, I began learning English as my fifth language – the only language that would make me think and speak entirely in words. English was slowly becoming my language of poetry.

In this poem, with his most elaborate yet simple language, Rumi speaks of a reed, either in the form of a flute or in its shape as a writing pen, that is lamenting its separation from its ground – like a human crying out in pain from being displaced from Heaven or the home of the heart. Had I not yet experienced exile deeply enough to understand Rumi? Or was it simply that I could not grasp the very simplicity of a language enchanted by poetry?

Was it simply because my mind had matured into that of an adult, or, more likely, because my soul was already that of a displaced and separated being, unable to comprehend the meaning? Or was it because I had finally arrived at Stanford, having left my home in Kabul in search of education and knowledge, hoping to understand every word Rumi spoke? Or perhaps it was the inevitable journey of self-discovery I had to undertake alone at twenty-one. A Sufi sheikh-mentor would have embraced the latter idea – would have taken me under their wings and made me feel even more dislocated and displaced in this earthly life. They would take the lead to give me another form of experiencing language that would transform my upcoming journey.

I found a sheikh-mentor to refine my pursuit of knowledge and my poetic language. Her name was Eavan Boland.

Eavan was an Irish poet. Her language of poetry was always English. She read and thought in English, and her phrases and the art of her speech were quintessentially English since birth. She claimed to have studied Greek and Latin, but I guess she would never have fully understood what it meant for someone like me – who had come to her with a limited command of English, the kind taught and learnt only in a classroom. I was far from knowing what she meant when she said, 'One day, you will be able to write in colloquial English. [...] Do you think you will ever be able to write that way?' Her head tilted slightly, and her eyes fixed on mine. She never waited for my answer. She did not need to know the answer. She always knew it. Then, she would change the subject. 'What about your Persian? Can you keep a conversation going? If you wrote a poem in Persian, would it be idiomatic?' She wanted to hear the answer to that. 'No, I am not able to...' 'Why?' she would ask, her curiosity piqued. 'And what about your dreams?' I explained that I never dreamt in any particular language. It was always images... With each conversation, I gradually became comfortable enough with Eavan to speak the truth of my life.

I told her that I grew up speaking the eastern dialect of Persian, known as Dari, which we are taught to believe is the purest form of New Persian – the one and only Persian (spoken to this day) that emerged from the fusion of Arabic and Middle Persian in the ninth century. However, I did not grow up learning the true essence of the language in everyday use. 'I think I understand poetry very well', I said. She responded, 'Ah, I see.' In the years that followed, I came to understand what Boland had been trying to ask me about idiomatic language – it was about the ownership of a language, the power that lies in simple speech.

I was one of those young girls living in the impoverished lanes of Quetta, Pakistan, where every corner seemed to hold a tumbledown yard, and in each yard, there were typically two to five rooms, with seven to nine people living as a family in each room. In those overcrowded rooms and desperately cramped yards, we never practised language through communication or conversation. To put it simply: war, violence, discrimination, displacement, migration and homelessness result in the erosion of the ability to communicate through language, let alone harness the power of speech. Even the women's corridors, where I roamed as a little girl, remained in total silence. Men held the power of language and over language, for it was their speech of politics, shared among other men, that commanded women to perform certain tasks. They occupied the centre of the yard, where the well was dug and a small shelter built for the men's gatherings. As young girls, we were passive recipients of language, born into this silence. That is why we never had the opportunity to ask or wonder what language could do – to demand, to change, or to challenge. We were never meant to know what it meant to truly understand language, let alone to speak it.

From that point onwards, in every meeting room and at every opportunity, Eavan would gently challenge me to take ownership of the language. That was when she asked me about translation. 'Perhaps we could read some Persian poets. Who would you like to read?' she asked, hoping I would name a female poet. I immediately mentioned one of the most renowned classical male Persian poets, Jami – a fifteenth-century Herat poet and scholar who held significant influence at the court of the Timurid Dynasty.

'Why him?' she asked, wanting me to consider whether his poetry made the world a better place. Of course, it did – he made the world better for himself and those other men around him, both within the court and beyond, and for generations of male readers to come. He was a male poet with a distinctly male gaze and vision. 'Are there any other poets that you can think of who made your world better?' Without hesitation, I named Rabia Balkhi, Forough Farrokhzad and Nadia Anjuman.

Our conversation began with a discussion about why these female poets mattered and how they spoke to me. I remember saying something along these lines: it was their use of language in a poetic way that allowed them to express themselves, and by reading them, I am granted the freedom to think, speak, and perhaps write my own poetry. I thought that was what poetry was about – that was what poetry did.

But these women poets were doing more than merely writing poetry. They were striving to become part of history and, in doing so, shape the history around them – both past and present. Though they remained publicly silenced for far too long, within their private spaces, they possessed the most liberated human voices.

That was where it all began. Eavan's encouragement to take ownership of my language started with translation, even before it became poetry. I translated a poem by Rabia, a poem by Forough and a poem by Nadia. These poets share something essential: their sense of freedom tears through the very fibre of poetic language.

The mother of Persian literature, Rabia, writing in the early tenth century, expressed:

> My invitation to you is a wish from your God
> to make you a lover –
> of a stone-hearted, unkind soul like yourself.
> To know the pain of love, the fear of desertion,
> you must bear sorrow.
> When you know the pain of this abandonment,
> you will know my worth.

As a poet and a woman with a secret pen, Rabia was punished and killed by society for her poetic talent. She wrote poetry in secrecy, in hidden places. The very thing that revealed her to the world – and ultimately led to her death – was poetry itself and her love of it.

In reading Rabia and translating her, I learnt to honour the private space where I am free to be a poet. My family lived in Kabul, and poetry was still dangerous. So, I quietly wrote my poems, page by page.

Forough, the modernist Persian poet, wrote with effervescent magic. Her words pierce the soul with truths spoken in the most beautiful language. She does not shy away from wounding or alienating the reader – her truth is more important than the comfort of conservative audiences. With Eavan, we read and translated the following brave words:

> I speak of the depth and length of the night,
> I speak of the deepness of the dark,
> and I speak of the vast darkness of this night.
>
> If you happen to come home tonight,
> o kind soul, bring me a lamp and a window
> so I may gaze upon the crowded, fortunate lane.

Mirroring Rabia and Forough, I anchored my translation journey in discovering more of Nadia's work.

> It is night, and poetry rains sparks in my moments,
> out of delight, it untangles the strings of my sound.
>
> What fire is it that so astonishingly offers me water,
> and breathes onto the climate of my body an
> aroma of the essence?
>
> I do not know from which mountain, what mountain
> of hope
> streams this fresh breeze to my terminal season.
>
> From the cloud, the light lands – it is that pure
> crystal light,
> that there is no need for my tears.
>
> The glints of my sigh make the star fall,
> into the heavens, the dove of my prayers nests.
>
> My unwanted tears on each line of His book,
> look, how with no excuse, they drop, my God.
>
> Letter by letter in a journal, and word by word into
> chaos,
> the judgment day has arrived with my stubborn
> silence.

Passing through the sea, dry mud, and a silken
touch,
all these – make me delightful,
at night, when poetry rains sparks in my moments.

Nadia had read both Rabia and Forough. Nadia somehow encompassed both in her language, her experience, the power of her speech, and, above all, her place in the history I shared as a little girl. Nadia lived under the first Taliban rule in the 1990s. Unlike me, roaming in silenced corners, Nadia's corner was a hidden cellar where poetry was allowed and practised. A sewing circle of Herat's women, she stitched word to word, crafting a dress that would shield her for the years to come.

Her first collection of poetry was published in 2005, at a time when the country was under American invasion. She became famous wherever Persian was read: in Iran, Afghanistan and Tajikistan. I saw her celebrated as a rising star. A few months later, I saw her on the news, murdered by her husband for continuing to write poetry.

Every Friday, after 3pm, Eavan and I would walk to the Union Square Starbucks, order our dark Americanos, and sit to discuss Nadia. By then, Eavan had become equally captivated by Nadia. Her questions always made me reflect on Nadia's poetry – on her role in shaping history, or how history had shaped her sense of poetry in the first place.

I never imagined that, over the next four years, spending two long hours each week with Eavan – discussing poetry, history, and the role of women in shaping both – would not only deepen my understanding of female Persian poets and their influence on our world, but also enhance my ability to read and translate Persian literature into English with greater freedom. It goes without saying that it was Eavan who helped me become a better poet by encouraging me to experiment with the languages I had grown up with but never truly owned as a young girl. She taught me how to inwardly translate those voices into English and express them through my own poetry. If not for colloquial English, I have written poetry that carries the echoes of several falling languages within one reed. And I am, without a doubt, part of the clan of writers who exist both between and within multiple languages. This is where the power of my simple poetic language resides and where my soul, fired by a love of languages, is reflected in the titles and poems I write – be it proper English or no English at all. It is, without a doubt, poetry.

Callimachus

ISOBEL WILLIAMS

'I'm writing versions of Callimachus's epigrams' sounds like 'I've got rabies' to judge by the way non-classicists react. I think people know Callimachus in one of three ways: a) not at all; b) inadvertently, via William Johnson Cory's translation of epigram 2, 'They told me, Heraclitus, they told me you were dead…'; c) because they are classicists, although he is not hard-wired into the syllabus.

He preached the gospel of *Reader's Digest* – cutting improves. Posterity misinterpreted this, and most of his works are lost or fragmentary; the Fourth Crusade was devastating for what had remained until then. He advised writers to take the road less travelled by, and to avoid sloppy pastiche of the epic (but this is not to diss Homer). Where the bee sucks (at the pure holy source), there suck I; the Euphrates carries trash. Also attributed to him is 'mega book, mega cock-up – mega bibilíon, mega kakon; μέγα βιβλίον, μέγα κακόν.'

Like many of his readers, I encountered him first via the Romans, loitering in footnotes. He occupies a good deal of Catullus's negative space – the vital bits you look for when drawing – and influenced Virgil, Horace, Ovid and Propertius (who called himself 'Callimachus Romanus'). He was colonised, translated into Latin in a different time, place and political set-up from his own.

He himself did PR, as a Hellenistic poet-librarian can, for the colonisers who were his employers, the second and possibly third Ptolemy. Their dynasty founded by one of Alexander the Great's Mycenaean generals, they declined to interbreed with the Egyptians they ruled, and needed to establish validity. One means of doing this was his long poem relating to customs and phenomena, *Aetia* (reasons, causes, justifications, origin stories, kingsplaining): Greek myth supplying context and continuity.

The Romans (who had more of his material than we do) favoured this poem, as well as his epigrams which come as an uncorseted relief after his fanned-out peacock's tail of intense learning – but in those longer works he was window-dressing for the elite, or for his scholarly émigré self in the Library of Alexandria at the western intellectual epicentre. Even one of his publicists has had enough: 'The hymns are very learned and artificial in style; the epigrams are good.' (At the time of writing this was on the Loeb website.)

The epigrams *are* good: confessional, amatory, admonitory, tragical-comical-historical-pastoral in a coffee spoon; the dead comment or complain through their grave markers; yearning for the caddish, beautiful boy is ungratified (you feel that Callimachus wasn't hot, unlike Catullus). Dedications are inscribed on votive offerings, from women begging to survive, and I voice those through a jaded auctioneer cataloguing a sale of what he unkindly calls temple tat.

Of course I'm scared of this very old material (the outer limits of his dates are about 310–235 B.C.). But a lot of auctioneers caution against wearing protective white gloves, especially when dealing with paper, because of a potential loss of dexterity. I prefer direct handling. Returning to Cory's epigram 2, the last line-break is

...ὁ πάντων
ἁρπακτὴς Ἀίδης...
– 'the all/robbing Hades'.

Cory has '... awake; / For Death, he taketh all away', but as he is a Victorian in the business of rhyming I don't object. I have 'the asset / Stripper Hades', with its whiff of the secret world of private equity, and maybe of the way City boys choose to entertain themselves after a deal, in a basement which is private for now. Translation is a treacherous transaction: there is profit and loss.

Multifarious Beast

OKSANA MAKSYMCHUK

When I was a child growing up in the Soviet Union on the brink of perestroika, my father taught me a poem titled, sentimentally, 'The Swans of Motherhood'. The poem, composed by a leading Ukrainian Soviet poet of the mid-fifties, Vasyl Symonenko, is a kind of exhortation to a male person of indeterminate age (the speaker calls him 'son'). The message (this is a poem with a message) is that 'you cannot choose a Fatherland' just as 'you cannot choose a mother'. The word for 'Fatherland' is a feminine noun, and placing it in the same sequence as 'mother' creates a metonymic connection, autochthonous myths of origin superimposing on natal determinism. What the poem does not say is that you cannot choose your language. Despite implicitly conforming to the homogenizing ideology of the Soviet project, whereby all the citizens of the twelve sister republics share a common tongue, this omission did not save the poet from getting brutally beaten up by the Soviet police in 1962, an event that is widely thought to have hastened his death the year after.

Is language a home, an origin, and a mother? Or is it an other, a lover, a stranger you learn to embrace and give in to, as a matter of choice? I came to wonder about this while I was growing up, every year a little more polyglossal, the umbilical cord which, presumably, tied me to the source stretching and separating in multiple directions, like a strange multi-headed beast, each with a split tongue of its own. There was something undisciplined and wild about this proto-Platonic creature, as if its existence made it difficult for a soul to embody an ideal of orderly composition, betraying a major feature of Plato's metaphysics: one is better than many.

The beast simile makes it seem that inhabiting multiple languages involves developing different selves, heterogenous and not easily reducible to a single coherent underlying identity. But that's only part of the picture. Different languages may also nourish different aspects of our varied and constantly changing souls, either because of who speaks them or writes in them, or whom we love, or the syntactical, semantic, grammatical, rhythmic, sonic, prosodic, phonetic, conceptual features of the languages themselves. As if answering our hunger for meaning, newness, and varied unsettled selfhood, languages offer themselves as sustenance. We don't just get tied up and roped into them: there's an active reaching, searching, pursuit. Perhaps, then, a complimentary analogy for acquiring languages is rooting, like a plant: casting tendrils in all directions, sensing sources of nurture and nourishment, somewhat blindly yet not indiscriminately?

I don't know what it feels like to be a tree, or a vegetable, though I suspect that these beings have rudimentary perceptual faculties, which enable them to set their parts – leaves, roots – in directed, seemingly intelligent motion in response to external stimuli. For a human being, the sensation that may poetically resemble this perceptual experience is wading through a body of water, where different currents meet without blending: now you're pulled, drawn and tugged this way, now that; now your body is warm and comfortable, and the next moment every muscle contracts as you enter an icy patch emanating from an invisible spring. Languages buoy you up, drag you down, engulf you completely and gently recede. Yet you're in water – in language – all along. You never leave this medium. You just float, or swim, or dive, or drown, struggling against the current, or going along with it, or letting it draw you in completely only to push you out to the surface once again. Then you start over.

Sometimes I find myself beached, like a whale. No language holds me, I am pushed out, I have no words. But the silence cannot last, unless you're alone in outer space, or cast out of society, or you've managed to become a hermit – and even hermits tend to converse: with beasts, with birds. Little by little, I am nursed back into language – by words of love, prayers and songs, insults, irreverent jokes.

So not two analogies, but three: umbilical cord, roots and tendrils, the mixing and unmixing of currents. As Protagoras, the first known relativist, wryly pointed out to Socrates: 'Indeed, anything at all resembles anything else in some way or other'.

Are we one, or many? Both, I suppose. Are languages one, or many? Again, both. Human languages, in particular, all resemble one another to some extent due to our shared cognitive faculties and the range of physiological capacities characteristic of our species. It would be odd to overemphasize the significance of the differences between any two natural human languages. Nevertheless, these differences exist. So do differences between individual humans, and between humans from different cultures, and humans during different historical periods. Yet we're all fundamentally the same, sustaining a range of the ways of life made possible by our physiology, psychology, the laws of nature, the material conditions on our planet. This is why human nature is an appropriate subject of a scientific study, as Thucydides too insisted in the first known attempt to write history involving no gods or miraculous happenings, making do with darkly clustered inventories of words and actions.

Despite our sameness, language is one mechanism for setting our group, tribe – and ourselves, as individuals – apart from others. We distinguish ourselves through language. Who is better qualified to give voice to this tendency than a poet? Through wild and unlawful episodes of expression and articulation, we poets individuate ourselves, make ourselves strangers to our own people and our own former and future selves. A poet is – often – someone who transforms what's familiar and comforting into something uncanny and disquieting, rendered in an alien idiom. To do this, poets must both be home and not home in a language. It's of secondary importance what language they learned to accomplish this in first.

The tongue your mother spoke to you as a child is a historical and socioeconomic contingency, and yet it's one that shapes you when you're at your most vulnerable, dependent. In Ukrainian, I am burdened by certain kinds of awareness, secretiveness and caution I do not experience in English. Language, in our political and social culture, was a marker of an identity on the basis of which you could end up in one of three categories: those who would be executed or dispatched to the camps; those who would be entrusted to toil faithfully for the collective good; and those who'd be spared for a time and observed closely. Potential defectors or saboteurs often ended up in the first group – the risks were considered too great for a society to absorb. To end up in the third group, you had to learn to pass with fluency, which had its own syntax, grammar and tone. Conformity and submission are not only survival strategies: they also make possible a certain kind of flourishing. Giving up your native language seemed like a small price to pay in exchange for the privileges that accrue with the recognition of your loyalty. If you kept your mother tongue, you flirted with the possibility of a hypersonic transfer from group three to a gulag, an internment camp, an execution chamber.

With the recent invasion of Ukraine, my Crimean husband and I darkly joke that every award, grant or honour bestowed on a Ukrainian author, filmmaker and artist is a kind of 'mark'; that the lists of awardees themselves are readily convertible into execution lists for enemy authorities if (when?) Ukraine falls under occupation. Why do we think this? In every occupied city, the torture chambers are filled with teachers of Ukrainian language, literature and history, in addition to the children and elders who voluntarily entered the self-organized territorial defence units to protect their towns and villages from the enemy advance. Speaking Ukrainian is considered as much a risk as stashing ingredients for a bomb or hoarding empty bottles and gasoline for Molotov cocktails. When Russian officials speak of disarmament and denazification, this is what they mean: the erasure of our difference. Speaking Ukrainian under occupation seems like a classic instance of civil disobedience. But it doesn't result in you getting fined or arrested, as a civic act might. You end up tortured, raped, killed.

Given the existential dangers involved in speaking my mother tongue, how dare I abandon it? Like any poet, I am drawn to extremes. Yet I'm not excessively impressed with the life of martyrdom and self-sacrifice. My father has always emphasized the importance of toiling on one's own soil, laying your talents on the altar of your own gods. I get it. Nobody else will clean up the house you were born in if you don't. And yet, with all the blood, and soiling, and clutter, you may decide that you'd rather direct your energies elsewhere. Even in Ukrainian, instead of trying to fill in gaps in our poetic tradition, as I did in my youth, I now luxuriate in writing around the absences and the silences, gingerly changing registers, shamelessly dragging in loot from other languages.

Poesis, like other forms of generative intimacy, is about striking a balance between freedom and constraint, proximity and distance. Just as you may feel too inhibited to have sex in your childhood bedroom, so you may feel too self-conscious to try out certain words, tropes, locutions or topoi in your native language. The opposite may also happen. Eros is known to feed on what feels forbidden and transgressive. Perhaps it's only in your native language that you can really come into your own? It may well depend on what kind of writer you are: what drives you, what turns you on and keeps you going.

In languages, as in other matters, it's never just about where you come from, but where else you've been, and where you'd like to be headed. My most enduring love affair is with English. This may have to do with the fact that it's the language in which I've had some of the most important friendships and love affairs of my life. To my child, it's a mother tongue. Yet there are some ten other tongues I've grown, to varied success, as sense-organs and appendages, enabling me to appreciate and admire the contingencies and particularities of grammar, the charming and vulnerable arbitrariness of words, the impurities and eccentricities of phonetics – these shaded folds and surfaces that make each linguistic landscape uniquely compelling, thrilling. Such ardour for mixtures – you might call it linguistic promiscuity – has freed me to be in language more bravely, and more lovingly, while always longing for some beyond: the threshold of meaning, the outer horizon of intelligibility.

Living between Languages

or *Eres de aquí, pero no eres de aquí*

PETER DAVIDSON

Please imagine a handsome drawing room in the New Town of Edinburgh, at dusk on an evening of freak snowfall. My aunt, still beautiful in her late seventies, sits on one side of the fireplace looking at the two tall windows through which snow can be seen falling heavily on the Water of Leith and the little neo-classical Temple of the Goddess of Health. I am sitting on the other side of the fireplace, up from the country and caught in Edinburgh by the new year snow, corduroy trousers and checked shirt, fleece waistcoat. Between the two windows is a birchwood secretaire from the first decade of the nineteenth century; my two elegant cousins, dark-haired sisters, are on the sofa facing the fire. We are talking about the snow and about how long it is likely to be before I can make my way home. At which point my aunt sneezes, and the three of us say in perfect unison, *¡Jesús, Maria, José!*

A decade later I was in the archaeological museum in Jerez (a rewarding museum in a nicely old-fashioned part of the town) and was asking for our tickets (my cousins were following on) and the genial people behind the desk, with genuine curiosity, asked the usual question of *where are you from*, adding *Eres de aquí, pero no eres de aquí*. (This is a phrase which haunts me.) Then my lovely cousins arrived, one sherry expert with a perceptible Andaluz accent, the other an artist with the elegant, whispering 'z' of her long Mexican residence, rekindling the question of how we had varying degrees of estuary accents (the estuary, that is, of the Guadalquivir) but were perhaps not exactly Spanish. So we said that we were descended from a family of Cadiz merchants, and Paula said she worked with wine in and around Andalucia, and all was smiles and free tickets. Which was for me the moment, comparatively late in life, when some modest competence in spoken Spanish suddenly, after decades, returned.

I made this visit to Jerez and Cádiz with my two cousins a few winters ago, an excursion which confirmed that we either spoke a dialect particular to three people, or perhaps we were all to some degree between the stools of language. By this time, I was in late middle age – my parents, following some insane theory widely believed in the third quarter of the last century, had stopped speaking Spanish to me (though not to each other) when I was about six, despite Spanish being my mother's first language, despite my father having a fair inheritance of American Spanish from his father who had built mighty, Conradian railroads in the high mountains of Argentina and Chile.

I found at university that, oddly, I was carrying with me a remarkably complete passive system of a language I hardly ever spoke. This passive knowledge never left me, so I found myself always able to read a language which only passed my lips on the rare occasions when I lost my temper so completely as to surprise myself with some phrase such as *por l'amor de Dios.*

There is a theory in circulation that the subject which someone chooses for an arts doctorate is often the question which they have to answer in their own lives. There is some truth in this, well at least for me. My own doctorate gathered and edited the poems and translations of an early modern Englishman who immersed himself in Baroque Spain, inventing in the process a kind of rarebreed, one-off 'English Gongoresque', which had no posterity. I read Gongora, Argensola and Quevedo in those years, also Lorca, and found that those poets (together perhaps with the proto-surreal neo-baroque of Apollinaire) seemed to be offering clearer examples of how to write verse in English than any English poet. I guess that Gongora and Lorca did for me what, say, Eliot or Elizabeth Bishop do for many people studying English who want to write verse.

I did get the degree in the end – not before some elderly male academic had fired across my bows a shot I should have heeded more – *I'm not wholly convinced that early modern Spain is a subject for serious study.* Indeed, this was fair warning, given that the study of Baroque Spain was viewed in Cambridge with the same suspicion that most manifestations of Catholicism and the Iberian world (synonymous of course) were viewed. Of course local conditions should again have given me a clue: those little, late blooms of the black legend flourishing in damp, unhealthy Fenland air, and the Roman Chaplain, Monsignor, a grandee from an old wine family, rumoured to be a godson of his late Catholic Majesty Alfonso XIII, who ran his Chaplaincy in sonorous Latin, as remote from the Anglican/Agnostic university as the Spanish Embassy Chapel in hostile Elizabethan London.

Those years did not end particularly well for me: in retrospect I was desperately naive to imagine that an intensive study of one Englishman's rarified translations from Spanish Baroque poetry and drama would charm, or even faintly interest, Cambridge examiners or employers. But I was launched on writing in a way that, certainly, was in some way directed by Auden and by place, but in terms of style, imagery and ultimately subject, haunted and delighted by Baroque Spain – and also, beyond the pillars with their plus ultra (real ones form the dock gates at Cádiz) by the whole, haunting, dream-invading glory of the *baroco de las Indias*.

When I started teaching, a slightly disconcerting phenomenon recurred: I would be lecturing in English, on British art or literature, and at the end of the lecture an exchange or visiting student would introduce themselves as coming from – let's say – Valladolid or Valencia and

– *Profesor, usted es español ¿no?* So even if my active command of the language was in deep sleep, I had retained a vocabulary of gesture and inflection specific enough to identify me as some kind of demi-Spaniard even from the back rows of a British lecture theatre. And for decades, while I concentrated on Latin, with Dutch and Italian as spoken languages, Spanish was always there, accompanying me in the shadows, rising to consciousness whenever I picked up a book in that tongue, spoke macaronically to my cousins.

There are a few curious side effects of this condition: an intense, niche dyslexia which can't distinguish which vowels should be in an English word adopted from Latin, if it differs from the parallel word in Spanish. And a total and abject inability to spell marmalade (I looked it up this time, I always have to.) A side effect I've occasionally observed in myself, *Cattolico ma non fanatico*, is to do with language and religion. I've never explored this, but I think if I did I would find that it's somehow easier to think about religion in Spanish than in English or Latin. I once dreamed a couplet of Holy Week poetry

Porfirizado de tu sangre,
Coronado de rosas morenas. . .

Visiting a Marian shrine, I've always found it natural to fall to my knees on the pavement in front of the image, once being told by a young Jesuit friend, *you can see Spain coming right out in you sometimes.* I still envy the relaxed and unfiltered attitude to religion which persists in parts of the Spanish south – the image of a street shrine to the suffering Christ in Jerez comes to mind, and with it the wonderfully casual ex-voto fencing masks and football shirts hung there in thanks for victories won, *per gracia ricevuta.* I am fond of sport and also fairly religious, but I cannot encompass the idea of my younger self unselfconsciously hanging up a votive scrumcap or Fives glove.

Enough anecdotes: I think there is perhaps one moderately interesting effect (or possibly, gift) of being brought up bilingual which has attended me all my life. Since I have carried alternative words for most commonly seen things around with me since I began to speak, I find that I can look at a thing and think of it (a table, a curtain, the first late-winter iris in their pot outside the study window) without attaching words to the objects in either Spanish, English or any other tongue. For me this is how things are: it is a condition which appears to foster a quick visual memory, but I'm never sure if it helps with language learning – I've always had some success in learning a new Romance or Germanic language, but have never made much headway with the difficult (if beguiling) Celtic tongues. What interests me most about this condition of *thinking in things* is that it is, quite possibly, the condition in which most of the Renaissance and early modern (I'd say *Baroque*) poets lived: Latin was always there as a recourse for them, and they could write as fluently in that ghost-tongue as in any vernacular. In that very emblematic age, that age of *concettismo,* how many of them thought in images between languages, and not in a language?

When I joined Campion Hall in Oxford, a Jesuit institution which opened its door to lay fellows about a decade ago, I had to introduce myself to the company gathered for dinner at the beginning of term. The best I could do was to say 'Well I am partly Scots and partly, I suppose, wine trade', which was instantly understood. Being 'wine trade' can be a sort of a nation, just like being a Jesuit is to belong to a transnational nation of polyglots. In another Oxford context I found myself offering the improvised suggestion to 'take an average of Perthshire and Jerez de la Frontera' (actually, it's Cádiz, but people have heard of Jerez). And, I now realise that more or less everything I've researched or written in my adult life has been governed by that consistent attempt to take an average of upland Britain and Atlantic Spain: studies of exiles, losers, recusants and Jacobites; studies of hybridity, exceptions, linguists and Jesuits. And I rejoice that I have come to harbour in the familial Jesuit Hall in Oxford, the most cosmopolitan college in the little Byzantium of the university, in the smallest cosmopolitan city on these islands. Campion Hall is one of the vanishingly few places where I don't have to explain anything, any more than I had to explain anything in the *Reál Colegio de Escoceses* in Salamanca, when I catalogued their pictures. And, all my writing and thinking has been attended by that odd, bilingual power of the *de facto* cosmopolitan, the faller between stools – to think in images of things and not (necessarily) in the words of any language. *Eres de aquí pero no eres de aquí.*

Bad Latin, Barbarous Inglishe and Broken French

Translation, Grace, and the Stone of Stumbling

VICTORIA MOUL

I'm learning Russian at the moment in order to read Russian poetry. My teacher is a woman in Kyiv, a war widow, who speaks to her older daughter in Russian and her younger daughter in Ukrainian. She is trying to decide whether she should leave. Our cleaning lady is also from Kyiv. She came to France with two young children. A couple of years ago when she first started working for us, she couldn't speak any French and we communicated via bits of English and her phone's translation app. But now she speaks French quite well and we no longer have to go via her phone. Since noticing my Russian textbooks and asking me about it, she speaks patient, slow Russian to me, complete with helpful gestures. The other day, when she arrived, I said 'dobrey dyen' (good morning in Russian) and then I asked her, in my broken Russian, how to say 'dobrey dyen' in Ukrainian, thinking that it would be polite to learn a few key phrases in her own language. 'Dobrey dyen', she replied.

When she came last week, I wanted to explain that I had an online meeting. I didn't know the Russian word, so I tried *meeting*. She looked puzzled and broke into a vigorous mime of someone waving a placard and shouting 'Putin, Putin', which took me by surprise. Next she tried a French word, *démonstration*, and the penny dropped. *Meeting* is Ukrainian (and perhaps Russian, too) for a *demo* – in the English sense; though actually the French word isn't really *démonstration* (you use that for the demonstration *of* something, like a method or technique), but *manif* (for *une manifestation*). My husband tells me that *meeting* used to have this sense in French as well.

My spoken French is quite good now but when we arrived it was fairly basic. A fortnight after we moved to France I became pregnant with Daniel, our youngest son, and immediately had to navigate an entire bureaucracy and health system in a language I only knew a bit – and it never seemed the right bits. (Being able to recite some Malherbe doesn't get you very far if you're trying to summarise your medical history.) I spoke a great deal of bad French in 2021 and 2022 with a large number of health professionals. One obstetrician – right in the middle of a rather horrible procedure, as I lay weeping with worry for the baby – suggested that I must be mistaken about being English, and was in fact German, since in his experience British people did not speak French. This made me reflect that the arrogance of surgeons is an international phenomenon, transcending language.

The other day I spent an hour interpreting at Daniel's crèche for a young couple who have recently arrived in France from Israel, neither of whom yet speak French. They speak Hebrew together; he speaks Russian with his family; they both speak good English. Daniel has made friends with their son, for whom crèche must be rather overwhelming. The staff report that they often speak English together and that Daniel, though he's only two, sometimes translates for him. Daniel has a rudimentary understanding of translation because there's a lilting refrain to our daily life that goes something like this:

Papa dit *pantalon*; Mummy says *trousers*. Mummy says *book*; Papa dit *livre*.

Daniel doesn't know what you mean if you ask him to 'translate', but if you frame the question in this way, he can often provide the answer. (If he doesn't know, he rolls his eyes around for a bit and then shouts *caca!* Which, as you have probably guessed, is French for *poo*, and the very acme of wit if you are two.)

Ann Loftus was born in Ireland in 1626. In 1640, when she was fourteen, her father died and she was sent to England. In 1653 she married Richard Barrett, had three babies very close together and then died of a fourth. In the Essex record office survives a notebook of hers, dating from the mid-1640s, when she was in her late teens, still a newcomer to England.[1] It contains a sequence of sixty-eight Latin epigrams of her own composition, several of which describe her love of Ireland and her horror of the war then engulfing both countries. Here are two of the epigrams from the first page:

> Hoc quem ciuiles funderunt sanguine dextrae.
> O! quantum terae vincere nunc potuit.
>
> *This is the blood which civil hands have poured.*
> *Oh! so much as now could o'erwhelm the land.*
>
> Nil teribilius quam bellum pergravius nil
> Nil contra pace est gratius et Melius.
>
> *Nothing more terrible than war, nothing graver;*
> *Nothing sweeter and more welcome than peace.*

Early modern England was, like the rest of Europe, a bilingual literary culture and short Latin verse part of its daily coin. Every schoolboy was taught to write Latin verse, and many men, even those who had no particular literary pretensions, continued to do so, for pleasure or politics, in adult life. The archives are filled with tens of thousands of such compositions, the great majority of

1 Essex County Record Office, MS D/DLF106.

them entirely unstudied – unedited, untranslated, unread. An entire forgotten literature of England.

All the same, Ann's verse is distinctive. She must have learnt the rudiments of Latin verse composition either alone, or with minimal guidance, since she makes many mistakes of a kind almost never seen even in schoolboy work. Early modern English spelling was notoriously flexible – people largely spelt words as they heard them – but this was not true at all of Latin, which had a very stable and internationally accepted orthography. As a result, you rarely see spelling mistakes in Latin verse of this period, but Ann's epigrams are full of them: in the two poems above, *terae* should be *terrae* and *teribilius* should be *terribilius*. She also doesn't seem to have known – as any schoolboy did – that if you're writing elegiac couplets in Latin, you're not supposed to end a line with a monosyllable. In fact, there are lots of basic problems with the Latin. *Hoc* doesn't agree with anything; *sanguine* should be *sanguinem*; even if *terae* is corrected to *terrae* it's still in the wrong case, it should be *terram*. Nor is the sentiment she expresses at all original: *civil blood makes civil hands unclean.*

Ann's epigrams are bad Latin. All the same, her attempt to write Latin verse, apparently entirely on her own initiative, suggests considerable intellectual ambition, and her couplets, all neat copies made in a careful hand, have an urgency of their own. Perhaps it's because her theme of exile, alienation and war seems to suit the imperfect expression of a partially mastered language. The brokenness becomes a kind of eloquence.

Adrian Schoell, a German Protestant immigrant recently arrived in London nearly a century before, in the 1550s, had the opposite experience to Ann. The product of a German grammar school, his Latin was excellent and reliable: indeed, his ability to write Latin verse to order appears to have been vital in his efforts to clamber out of the servant class he briefly occupied and into respectability – acquiring a patron, becoming a schoolteacher and eventually a clergyman. To start with, his Latin compositions are almost purely topical, either autobiographical or commissioned, with occasional translations from German, presumably his mother tongue.[2] After a while – perhaps not coincidentally, during the year in which he courts and then marries his wife, Juliana Raye, an Englishwoman – he starts sometimes to translate English poems into Latin.

Only at the very end of his life, in 1592 (he died in 1599) do we find him venturing some English verse of his own, a companion poem to a series of Latin epigrams commemorating the death of one Joan Wats, titled 'My meter [i.e. a poem of my own composition] in Barbarous Inglishe':

Here lyeth Joan Wats of breath bereft, In godlie liffe upright.
Accordinge state none like she left, To poore and needie whight.
In rulinge householde most skilfull, To profite best she mate.
About strangers likewise carefull And neighbours: to voide hate

If Ann's epigrams are bad Latin verse, this is surely pretty bad English. But Schoell could translate *into* Latin beautifully, and several of his best compositions are translations – the effort of recasting English lyric into Latin seems to have prompted him towards a grace and concision that his more discursive original poems tend to lack. Here are a few stanzas from a 1564 Latin translation of an English moralising lyric. The poem is in sapphic stanzas, a form pioneered in Latin by Catullus and Horace, but used widely in the mid-sixteenth century for formal moralising, religious or political verse.

Lingua nullius, mea nec, referre
scit deo coram miserûm patrono
lugubres soles, gemitusque crebros,
quos traho tristis.

Me dolet natum, quoties maligni
tramite a uero faciles recedunt.
Spes tamen mentis solidum leuamen
me fouet usque.

Nil homo cum sis, nisi ceu cadauer
putidum, (dixi), fimus atque puluis:
ne tuis speres meritis beari, ast
sanguine Christi.

[. . .]

Regibus, fidas minime, caducis,
Lex quibus fas, est, regimen Tyrannis.
his licet celsis, humilis piusque
prestat abunde.

Schoell conscientiously includes a copy of the poem he is translating: a politically pessimistic piece of moralising, written in iambic pentameter but with heavy alliteration, which is entirely typical of English verse in the 1560s. But though it's very like dozens of other English lyrics of the period, this particular poem has apparently not, as it happens, survived in any other source, so Schoell's translation of it has effectively preserved it twice: in its Latin version, and in the original, which would otherwise have been lost. These are the English stanzas corresponding to the verses quoted above:

1.
The doolfooll dayes that I drive on in dole,
The sobbes, the syghes that I doe fatche in sole,
To hym that maye eche cause and case redresse,
No tonge can tell, nor I myselff expresse.

2.
I wyshe I wer vnframd, not born at all,
To see the godlie wayes declyne and fall:

2 All transcriptions of Schoell's verse are taken from his surviving notebook, Corpus Christi College, Oxford, MS 324.

But alwayes hope, wich neuer fayles at neede
Is euer prest, my hongrie soele to feede.

3.
O man I sayd, what art thou in thy lust,
But dead, stinking caryon, dorte, dunge and dust:
Then trust not by thy woorkes to win the rase,
But by the blud of Christ to purchase grace.

[. . .]

5.
Put not thy trust in kinges, for they are vayn
Theyr lawe is lust, in Tyrannie they rayn:
And when they thinke at hyghest for to be,
A iust mean man is better, then is he.

Schoell was a devout and determined Protestant, and this venture into translation from English was perhaps prompted by the distinctly Protestant emphasis of the poem ('Then trust not by thy woorkes to win the rase / But by the blud of Christ to purchase grace'). Luther had insisted, in a departure from previous mainstream Christian theology, that divine grace was not dependent in any way upon human action. In his translation, Schoell removes the metaphor of a race and supresses that contentious word *grace* entirely. His Latin version, *ne tuis speres meritis beari, ast / sanguine Christi*, keeps it simple: 'Do not hope to be blessed because of your good deeds, but / [only] by the blood of Christ'.

Translation was a hot topic in the mid-sixteenth century, and one of Schoell's most ambitious compositions, running to many hundreds of lines, is a defence of the translation of scripture into the vernacular. (The poem itself, somewhat ironically, is in Latin.) At one point, he compares the man trying to follow a language of which he knows only very little to a blind bird pecking around a granary:

Ales caeca uelut circum granaria pascens
semina de multis uix legit ore duo.
Saepe potest rostro nullum contingere, multa
quae legeret, uisa si frueretur inops.
Sic euangelij quando hauserit aure tenorem
romanum, studijs turba perita minus:
Vix casu uerbum sitiens intelligit unum,
perceptura satis nota ubi lingua foret.

Like a blind bird feeding around the granary,
of the many seeds it barely picks up two.
Often it lights upon none at all, although many
are there to be chosen, if only he could see.
So too, when an uneducated crowd drinks in the sense
of the Gospel in the Roman form [i.e. in Latin]:
for all their thirst they scarcely chance to understand,
a single word, though it would be clear enough in a language they knew.

This fine simile is so effective, I think, because it suggests not only the frustration of incomprehension and the hunger to understand, but also the overwhelming impression of *abundance* when you are surrounded by a language you do not speak. Schoell is not thinking here of picking your way, word by word, through a written text, looking up almost everything. The comparison is to conversation: when you muster your best French or German to ask a simple question at the pharmacist, and receive in return a flood of impassioned commentary and advice. So much information, right there! But all you can do is peck vainly at the odd word as it goes by. Schoell wrote this poem in 1555, in his first year in the country, when his English was by his own admission limited. He knew what it was like to be that blind bird surrounded by unseen grain.

Thomas More, a stout defender of Catholicism and a man quite keen on the burning of Protestant heretics like Schoell, nevertheless also defends the translation of the Bible into the vernacular. On this point, the two agree – and in fact it is Schoell, not More, who calls English *barbarous*, a claim More explicitly denies:

> For as for that oure tonge is called barbarouse, is but a fantasye. For so is, as every learned man knoweth, every strange language to other. And if they would call it barren of words, there is no doubt but it is plenteous enough to express our minds in anything whereof one man hath used to speak with another. Now as touching the difficulty which a translator findeth in expressing well and lively the sentence of his author – which is hard alway to do so surely, but that he shall sometime minish either of the sentence or of the grace that it beareth in the former tongue – that point hath lain in their light that have translated the Scripture already either out of Greek into Latin or out of Hebrew into any of them both, as by many translations which we read already to them that be learned appeareth.[3]

More acknowledges the limits of translation. Anyone who translates finds that he or she must sometimes '*minish* [= diminish] *either of the sentence or of the grace that it beareth in the former tongue*'.

Sentence here doesn't mean the syntactical unit of a sentence, but its *meaning* – borrowed from Latin *sententia*. Usually when More writes about the *sentence and something* of a text, he uses the phrase *sentence and understanding*, that is, 'the meaning and the interpretation'. Here, though, thinking specifically about the challenges of translation, he pairs *meaning* with *grace*. In Latin, *gratia* means (among other things) beauty or elegance; on that basis, we might translate it here as something like *style*. As anyone who translates regularly knows, it is indeed very difficult to render both the meaning of a text and its distinctive style and aesthetic appeal. But *grace* is of course a theological term too, and a key word in the *Dialogue Concern-*

3 *Dialogue Concerning Heresies* (1530), 3.16. Spelling and punctuation modernised.

ing Heresies. More insists – *contra* Protestants like Luther and Schoell – that what we do by our own actions plays a part in the eliciting and receipt of divine grace.

It's hard to think of a less fashionable English text than More's *Dialogue Concerning Heresies*, a polemic that endorses the most dreadful form of execution for unremitting heresy, and which is written in a conversational form of English as it was spoken in the 1520s – there is no punctuation in the original apart from the virgule (/), which is more like a breath mark than modern punctuation. More than anything else, the dialogue is about *speech* – the power and danger and beauty of talking to one another – and about language as it is spoken, in the mouth and on the tongue, as it is chammed ('chewed', one of his favourite words) and corrupted and turned to wit or wisdom. It is one of the great love poems to the English language.

As he turns to consider the risks of translation into the vernacular, More makes a remarkable comparison between translation and the divine venture of the incarnation itself:

> Whereof I would not, for my mind, withhold the profit that one good, devout unlearned layman might take by the reading [of scripture] – not for the harm that a hundred heretics would fall in by their own willful abusion; no more than our Saviour letted [*refused*] for the weal [*benefit*] of such as would be, with his grace, of his little chosen flock, to come into this world and be *lapis offensionis, et petra scandali* (1 Peter 2), 'the stone of stumbling, and the stone of falling' – and ruin to all the wilful wretches in the world beside.

Speaking another language – indeed, speaking at all – is risky and difficult; it never works perfectly; you can be misunderstood; the pain of incomprehension and imprecision is real; and others might take your words and do wrong by them. But each time we try to reach across that divide, however ineffectually, between the word and its meaning, we are become a *lapis offensionis et petra scandali*, a little incarnation; a moment of grace; and the ruin of the wickedness of the world, in all its awful variety.

On Translating Plato's *Symposium*

ARMAND D'ANGOUR

As an undergraduate at Oxford in the late 1970s I was mesmerised by Plato's *Symposium*, which was an examination set text in Greek. The brilliant *mise-en-scène* involving a group of men discussing the meaning of love – or, more strictly, speaking in praise of Eros, the god of love – enlivened the way the topic was presented and seemed to align it with my adolescent preoccupations. In particular, I found (as many do) the speech of the comedian Aristophanes towards the centre of the dialogue to be immensely seductive. He spins a tale about the way original human beings were once duplicates of what we are now, consisting of male-male, female-female, or male-female creatures with two bodies – four hands, four legs, and so on. So powerful and self-satisfied were they that Zeus, chief of the Olympian gods, decided to chop them in half ('as if slicing an egg with a hair') so as to weaken them. 'When the original form had been cut in half' (I translate) 'each half desperately clung to its other half, and they threw their arms around one another in their desperation to graft themselves back on to each other.' Love, Aristophanes concludes, is what 'draws us back to our original nature and seeks to make one out of two and so repair human nature'. This desire to be complete and whole, then, is what Eros inspires in human beings.

I found this comically contrived myth meaningful and enchanting, and in the conviction that a girlfriend – not herself a classicist – also would, I presented her with Benjamin Jowett's lively Victorian translation of the dialogue. She tried to read it but confessed that she could not make headway with it. She never even got as far as Aristophanes's speech, because she found the style heavy-going and the train of thought barely intelligible. To me her reaction was surprising and disappointing, and at the time I scoured the translation to try and understand if the fault might be in Jowett's English rather than in Plato's Greek. Yet to my eyes the former seemed, as it still does, as bold and readable as the latter was clever, varied and stimulating.

Decades later, as I embarked on my own translation of the *Symposium*, I recognised clearly that the problem lies largely in the dialogue's cultural foreignness and alien intellectual assumptions. A discussion of love that is at the same time a debate about the nature of a god or spirit, in which erotic liaisons are discussed mainly in masculine and homoerotic terms, and which is set in an Athenian world of constant warfare and urgent philosophical inquiry rather than domestic relationships and popular psychology, will struggle to appeal to modern readers of conventional and predominantly heterosexual romantic inclinations. However, Plato was not writing only for men and soldiers, or only about love between men: the principles evoked by the participants in the symposium, not least by the figure of a woman, Diotima, who voices the doctrine of love presented by Socrates, undoubtedly have broad relevance to questions of desire, erotic satisfaction and loving relationships.

The lessons of the dialogue must, however, be drawn out from their largely unfamiliar background, and to do so the translation should aim to be as immediate and lucid as it would have seemed to an ancient reader. How, though, is one to translate not just the words but the intentions behind them, not just the expressions but the connotations they would have had for ancient readers (people of regular intelligence, that is, not practised philosophers)? In my *How to Talk about Love* (Princeton, 2025), I have chosen passages from the main sections of the *Symposium* – each of the seven speeches which essentially comprise the dialogue – and have given them brief introductions, so that the reader can understand the context within which each is couched. Plato has designed the dialogue with cunning skill so that each speech builds on or complements the last, and it is hugely rewarding to detect him putting the various elements in place so that they can be drawn together into a satisfying whole – rather as Aristophanes is made to describe Apollo's post-surgical reshaping of the newly-cut human beings: 'he pulled the skin together from all sides, the way you pull a purse shut with drawstrings'.

One particular cultural practice that posed difficulty for the purpose of my translation was the ancient Athenian custom of *paiderastia*, the relationship conducted between a man and a male teenager that, perhaps at best, aimed purely to benefit the latter in terms of social education and intellectual improvement. The fact that these relationships were often, if not necessarily, sexual was a cause of some discomfort to the Greeks, and in this dialogue the concern ultimately leads to the idea that what we call 'Platonic' (i.e. non-sexual) love might be a better and more noble course of action. However, the Greek words *erastēs* ('lover') and *erōmenos* ('beloved'), used to describe the two participants in such relationships, had specific hierarchical connotations: the former was always the older, more experienced, man, the latter the younger, physically appealing, object of his affection and desire. We might today talk about two 'lovers', or about a man and his 'boyfriend', 'sweetheart', or 'partner'; but these terms are romantic rather than descriptive, and do not maintain the straightforward specificity regarding age and status that is needed in at least three of the speeches for the speaker's point to be made. To use terms that preserved the distinction, I decided (somewhat reluctantly) that they had to remain 'lover' and 'beloved'.

Perhaps the most obvious difficulty in translating the *Symposium*, however, is the word *erōs* itself. Sometimes it is used as a purely abstract term to mean 'love' or 'desire'; sometimes it refers directly to the god Eros; but much of the time it hovers deliberately and ambiguously between the two. 'Love has enormous power', claims the physician Eryximachus; 'Love is the glory of gods and men, the best and brightest leader', rhapsodises the poet Agathon; 'Love is birth in the beautiful, as regards both body and soul', states the clever Diotima, leading her interlocutor Socrates to exclaim, as well he might, 'That needs an interpreter! I don't understand it.' Diotima goes on to explain that a lover is inspired by beauty to become creative: in the presence of, or in association with, someone we find beautiful we will produce 'offspring', whether actual children from sexual union, or new ideas and perceptions from intellectual intercourse. In the search for a pithy definition, Socrates must be satisfied with Diotima's avowedly obscure 'birth in the beautiful' (*tokos en kalōi*); and though the translator will often want to make clear what seems clear enough in the Greek, one also needs to preserve the sense of mystery and obscurity that arises when what is said is not as easy to grasp.

from *Magadh*

SHRIKANT VERMA

Selected by Stefan Tobler

The publisher Stefan Tobler writes: In Shrikant Verma's masterpiece *Magadh*, first published in Hindi in 1984 and to be published in Rahul Soni's English translation in the UK for the first time this October by And Other Stories, a chorus of narrators – commoners, statesmen, nameless wanderers – mull on the histories of ancient cities and kingdoms (including Magadh), their rise to splendour, their decline and eventual fall. Some critics sometimes view the book as one long poem, others as a collection of poems.

Magadh

Listen horseman, where's Magadh?
I've come
from Magadh
I must go to
Magadh

Where
do I turn?
North or south,
east or west?

Here I see Magadh,
here it disappears –

just yesterday
I left Magadh
just yesterday
Magadh's people
told me not to
leave Magadh
I gave my word –
I'd be back
before sunrise

But there is
neither Magadh nor Magadh
You too have been searching
brothers,

this is not the Magadh
you've read about
in books,
this is the Magadh
that you
like me
have lost

The People of Magadh

The people of Magadh
are sorting the bones of the dead

Which ones are Ashoka's?
And Chandragupta's?
No, no,
these can't be Bimbisara's
they are Ajatashatru's,

the people of Magadh say
and shed
tears

It's natural

those who've seen a man alive
only they
will see him dead
those who haven't seen the living
how can they see the dead?

Just yesterday
the people of Magadh
saw Ashoka
going to Kalinga
returning from Kalinga
Chandragupta riding his horse to Takshashila
Bimbisara
in tears
Ajatashatru
flexing his muscles

The people of Magadh
had seen
and they
can't forget
that they
had seen

those who
can no longer
be found

Corpses in Kashi

Have you seen Kashi?
Where
corpses come and
corpses go
by the same road.

And what of corpses?
Corpses will come,
corpses will go –

ask then, Whose corpse is this?
Rohitashva's?
No, no,
all corpses can't be Rohitashva

His corpse
you'll recognise from a distance
and if not from a distance, then
from up close –
and if not from up close,
then it
can't be Rohitashva

and even if it is
will it make a difference?

Friends,
you have seen Kashi,
where
corpses come and
corpses go
by the same road.

And this is all you did –
made way
and asked –
Whose corpse is this?

Whoever it was,
whoever it wasn't,
did it make a difference?

Justice in Kashi

The council has been dismissed
Councillors, let's go

What had to happen happened
Why then the long faces?
Why this anxiety?
What are we afraid of?

We did not judge –
merely nodding in agreement is not judgement
We didn't even give it a moment's thought
The debaters debated
what did we do?

What's our fault?
We don't call the council
We don't judge
We come to Kashi
once a year
to say only this
The council is unnecessary
everyone has already been judged
before they are born

Kosambi

Vasavadatta asks,
What came
before
Kosambi?

Vasavadatta!
Before Kosambi
there was only
Kosambi,

after Kosambi
there is only
Kosambi
In return for
Kosambi
you can get
only Kosambi
Searching for Kosambi
Vasavadatta
has reached
Kosambi

Hastinapur

Consider
a person
who comes to Hastinapur
and says
No, no, this can't be Hastinapur!

Consider
a person
left all alone –
why should he care when the Mahabharata
was fought?

If you can,
consider
Hastinapur,
for which
time and again
a Mahabharata is fought,
and no one cares
except that person
who comes to Hastinapur
and says,
No, no, this can't be Hastinapur!

The Customs of Hastinapur

I say again
without dharma, there can be nothing –
but no one
listens to me.
It isn't the custom to listen in Hastinapur –

those who hear
are either deaf
or have been appointed
to turn a deaf ear

I say again
without dharma, there can be nothing –
but no one
listens to me

Listen or not then
people of Hastinapur! Beware!
In Hastinapur
your enemy is being raised: Thought –
and remember
these days it spreads like the plague:
Thought.

My Mother Tongue, My Fatherland

ZINOVY ZINIK

1.

Like many of my contemporaries of similar background, I speak and write in two, if not three, languages, all three of them with the same accent – my foreign accent. You can make yourself unnoticeable in a pub: casual dress and unobtrusive manners would do the trick. But once you open your mouth asking for a pint, your cover is blown. The accent betrays you. An inevitable question pops up from a friendly face standing next to you at the bar: 'Where are you from?' I usually assume that the guy is not Professor Higgins; so, to cut the long game of guessing short, I find it easier to reveal the facts: I was born and grew up in Russia. I could have elaborated and explained that I am a Moscow-born assimilated Jew; I left the Soviet Union fifty years ago (I was stripped of my Russian citizenship as a condition of my departure); I went straight to Israel where for a year I ran a student theatre in the University of Jerusalem; then, while I was staying in Paris with my French publisher, Her Majesty the Queen's government invited me to cross the Channel to join the BBC World Service and settle down in Britain. Ten years later, I became a British citizen. But my interlocutor interrupts me: 'How are Russians in London doing?' he asks. Which Russians has he in mind? Russian oligarchs? Bohemian artists? Illegal migrants? Vodka merchants? 'I mean the Russian community in London', he elaborates.

There are plenty of Russians in London. But no community. Russians used to be wary of each other, suspicious of the other's dubious past, and found it difficult to get collectively together. In the seventies, even if there were a 'Russian community', I would have done my best to stay away from it. I hadn't parted with the place of my birth to get stewed in the stale, suffocating atmosphere of small groupings of my former compatriots. And who, in my interlocutor's imagination, does this 'Russian community' consist of? Bearded Tolstoys and Dostoevskys around the table in the company of Doctor Zhivago and Anna Akhmatova, drinking vodka out of a samovar, watching Sputnik in the night sky under the accompaniment of Gypsy guitars and then murdering each other for the sake of some Radiant Future? Russians in the London of the seventies were an odd exotic bunch. London was not yet a refuge for the bright young asylum seekers, well-educated cosmopolitans who had recently run away from Putin's autocratic Russia.

When people use the word community, they immediately form in their minds some ethnic clichés and shibboleths that are associated with such an entity. The moment you mention your foreign origin, you fall into a trap of being stereotyped accordingly. That's the main reason why some of us are still reluctant to mention their place of birth. At an unfamiliar gathering, I tend not to disclose my Russian origin, for fear of being mistaken for an unemployed oligarch. People tend to resort to national stereotypes, popular images of the country in question – it helps to enliven the conversation and get to know you better. People want to know whom they are dealing with and, if you happened to be in Northern Ireland, which God you do not believe in, Catholic or Protestant.

We are urged nowadays to feel proud of our ethnic origin and ancestral culture. This attitude very frequently implies that our ethnic origin defines our psychological profile – a notion that essentially is not very different from an obsolete Marxist conviction that our social origins define and determine the mode of our daily life, even quotidian aspects of our relationships with the outside world.

In Britain, where the culture of village communities is deeply rooted and even applied in judging personal character, it is difficult to avoid the question: 'Where are you from?' The Nietzschean dichotomy of Being or Becoming is constantly at play. Understandably, people are curious about new places and personalities, family habits and exotic cuisine. I don't mind being asked, 'Where do you come from?', unless I have a reason to suspect that what I have really been questioned about is: 'When are you going back where you belong?'

I'm neither denying my Russian inheritance, nor am I going to rewrite my past, in Stalin's fashion, to fit the current vision of the future – my future in London. Britain has cured me of the fear of an encounter with alien aspects of life – the Soviet fear of the unfamiliar. That's why during my accidental encounter with a fellow drinker at the bar, having detected a particularity of his own accent, I responded to his questioning in the same fashion: 'And where are you from, mate?' I asked. 'I am a Londoner', he answered promptly. His accent, though, was not that of a London cockney. 'But where were you born? Where did you grow up?' I persisted. 'In Ireland', he answered. 'How is the Irish community in London doing?' I asked.

I hit the bull's eye. He expressed some degree of puzzlement and asked me what I meant. I mentioned a few stereotypically Irish things that come to mind automatically: Guinness and whiskey, the Irish jig, IRA bombing. 'I left Ireland years ago and have nothing to do with these stereotypes', he said. 'Why then do you interrogate me about the Russian community in London?' I asked. After a pause, a confession followed: 'You see, my Jewish great-grandmother escaped pogroms in Russia before the Revolution and settled down in Ireland. I'm curious about my identity.'

2.

Should I have told my accidental interlocutor, a wandering Jew from Ireland, that after a year of running a student theatre in Jerusalem, I had become so fluent in Hebrew that, for a while, I felt as if Hebrew was my native tongue – despite the fact that neither the sound of this ancient language, nor a word of Yiddish, had ever been heard among my parents or grandparents? During my first months in Paris and London, after a year in Jerusalem, if somebody happened to ask me something casual in Russian, I automatically replied in Hebrew. The sound of Hebrew nowadays, though, at the time of the catastrophic events in Gaza, might draw undesirable attention on the streets of London and destroy the atmosphere of conviviality even among close friends. The same antagonistic reaction is only expected nowadays if someone were to start speaking Russian in the company of Ukrainians.

Once the foreign accent is detected, it colours the conversation politically. People try to guess your tribal, social, ethnic and religious affinities, and want to identify you as part of a certain collective, myth, mythology. Writers are alert to it and afraid to be identified with a 'wrong' national history. An author's personal life story or odd political views sometimes overshadow the author's creation. Some of us find the music of Richard Wagner or books by Louis-Ferdinand Céline unpalatable because of their antisemitic posturing; while Rudyard Kipling with his songs of the British Empire is *persona non grata* on the shelves of some progressive liberal libraries.

Solid as ever the popular image of classic Russian poets – a chosen few confronted and persecuted by an aggressive tyrannical mob of Stalinists – the same image as had been created a century ago by Isaiah Berlin in his 'Meetings with Russian Writers'. A century later, those few authors who have moved abroad, outside Russia, who are keen on adapting themselves to a new cultural milieu and capable of the dramatic transformation of their mode of thinking, regard a possibility of changing the language of self-expression as a mark of liberation from the doom and gloom of their past. But they enter the new literary world with a heavy baggage of old stereotypes associated with their fatherland.

For some writers, though, the haunting images of the national past resurface at unpredictable times and places, regardless of the language of expression, native or foreign. Germans who had survived and got liberated from the Nazi regime are an apt example. Such a past pervades one's life like cancer, which is as difficult to eradicate as your foreign accent. The language you use makes you inadvertently share some of the national myths associated with that language. Paul Celan, in the words of his translator Michael Hamburger, created his own poetic language, because he believed that his German should not be identical to the language of those who had murdered everyone and everything that had been dear to him. Should we feel ashamed of our mother tongue?

Still, one can manage to transcend the haunting past by different means. We change the themes of our fiction, the names of our characters, and avoid shibboleths of the traditional style in order to cover up and get away from our national background. Joseph Conrad, born in the part of Poland annexed by Russia, did this by setting his first novels in English at sea – a territory of superimposed multiculturalism of seafarers. Vladimir Nabokov transformed his nostalgia for the years of idyllic youth in Russia into an erotic image of the American nymphet.

Some radical exiles reject their native language in order not to feel an accomplice to the crimes of their national history, real or imagined. Other bilingual swingers would say they are just inspired by the authors of antiquity who, regardless of their motley ethnic origins and nationalities, used Greek or Latin as universal languages of intellectual and artistic exchange. But there is no neutral universal language such as Latin in use any longer. Liberated from the guilty burden associated with our national history by switching to another language, the author, through the use of this foreign language, gets psychologically entrapped by the crimes and misdemeanours of the adopted nation.

*

Am I getting a bit obsessive with this theme? Some remarkable authors of English fiction, who became professional expats, didn't feel any emotional necessity to switch into the foreign tongue of their adopted country. The Canadian Mavis Gallant lived happily in Paris to the end of her life and, without any qualms, kept on publishing her short stories in the *New Yorker*. Did Samuel Beckett, as some of his biographers suggested, periodically switch to French because of an urge to unburden himself from an oppressive past – his Irishness, his linguistic bond with the ancestors, Irish history, which, according to James Joyce, was 'a nightmare from which I'm trying to awake'? In a foreign language you can say something you would be ashamed of in your native tongue. You get rid of the fear of self-exposure – the fear of yourself – by hiding your intimate thoughts in a foreign verbal milieu. Because of a hint of cowardice and treachery in the act, such a liberation from the nightmare of national history doesn't come without a sense of guilt – as if by switching to another language you are renouncing your mother tongue.

I had a conversation on the subject with Mavis Gallant, who was bilingual – in English and French – since her childhood. She categorically rejected such a psychoanalytical relationship of Beckett's writing in French with his Irish background. 'By writing in French, Beckett didn't try to avoid his Irishness', she said. 'He just wanted to try the strictness of a lesser vocabulary and grammar rules.' (I'm quoting from a recording I had made of my conversation with Gallant in Paris in 1988.) She told me that she had never thought of changing to French in her fiction because she had never believed that her decision to settle down in France was prompted by her alienation from her Canadian past and English language.

Does this dilemma of abandoning the mother tongue for a foreign language exist only for the authors who have emigrated or got exiled from the countries with a problematic national history? The most exemplary linguistic cases of that kind, for me as a Russian, are, of course, those of Vladimir Nabokov and Joseph Conrad.

Transition from Russian to English was easier for Vladimir Nabokov, because English was the language he occasionally spoke at home in his childhood. In his twenties, he graduated from Trinity College, Cambridge, before taking up a teaching job in America. 'My head says English, my heart, Russian, my ear, French', Nabokov famously quipped, in protest to any kind of ethnic labelling. He was echoing, of course, Charles V, Holy Roman Emperor, who had sorted out his multilingual universe in the following way: 'I speak Spanish to God, Italian to women, French to men, and German to my horse'. And yet, Nabokov's pronouncements on the origins of his creativity in English are frequently interspersed with self-reproach and regrets over leaving one's native tongue and literature.

The development of Joseph Conrad as a British author looks much more enlightening to me, more instructive to everyone who begins a new life of writing in another language. Joseph Conrad (born Józef Teodor Konrad Korzeniowski, 1857–1924), was a Pole born in the Ukrainian town of Berdychiv. When Conrad was four, his father, a Polish aristocrat, a revolutionary who had conspired against the Russian rule of Poland, was exiled from Berdychiv to Vologda, a northern Russian town. Technically, therefore, Conrad was at the time a Russian citizen. That's why, when he was looking for a job as a sailor in Marseille, he was only temporarily employed by the French. (The British did not care about passports.) These Russian aspects of Conrad's biography are cherished by those Russian historians who are always happy to enlarge the borders of Russian literature. I have no doubt that Conrad knew Russian well – his literary allusions to Russian literature (such as, for example, a borrowing from Dostoevsky in his novel *Under Western Eyes*) were self-evident. But he never, as far as I know, let his knowledge of Russian be known to the public.

The children of the multicultural Soviet Union spawned many Russian literatures in the Russified Soviet Republics, from Tallinn to Tashkent. Yet, the inclusion of Joseph Conrad into this literary empire, simply because he was born in a Russian town, would have made him turn in his grave. If we define the identity of an author by the family's past, not by the author's language, we should enlist Saul Bellow (born as Solomon Belov) as a Russian novelist, too. His parents were Russian immigrants to Canada. Kipling will be, accordingly, an Indian writer. The big problem would be to sort out the Russian identity of Pushkin, who had black African ancestors. He never travelled abroad but wrote first drafts of his poems in French. Should we call him a French poet of African origin born in Russian exile? And, instead of being called a Russian author who lives in Britain, should I be known as a British author writing in Russian?

Conrad's choice of the English language had been prompted by his instinctive desire to get away from Russian cultural dictatorship. His second language, as for many Polish aristocrats, was French. But wasn't it an urge to have his new British identity accepted publicly that made trips to Paris so enjoyable for Conrad? Fluent as he was in French, his Polish origin would have been revealed through his accent; while his Polish accent in English would pass unnoticed among the French. The French might have thought his English was impeccable. There, in his attire of tweeds and brogues, he looked like a thoroughbred country gentleman.

Your native tongue, though, always lurks nearby and catches you unawares. In his memoirs, Conrad's son Borys wrote that when unwell or under emotional strain, Conrad's mispronunciations became more marked. Borys tells us how shocked he was when Conrad, after a medical check-up, quoted to his son what the doctor had said: 'Of course you are dying'. Back at home, Conrad's wife explained to the son: 'Don't worry, dear. He didn't say "You are dying", he said "iodine", he always pronounces it "uredyne"'. During the severe attacks of gout, in a semi-conscious state, Conrad swore in Polish, returning to his native land, as it were.

3.

I think it was from Beckett – most probably, from Beckett's trilogy – that I picked up the idea that we are forever verbally enslaved by our parents' manner of speech, which we instinctively imitate. The parental speech already contains an innate duality. Our bilingual nature, our verbal duality is lodged in our minds from the day of our appearance in this world. I can share with you here my own home-brewed mock-psychoanalytical theory of that verbal duality.

The first human sounds we learn are pronounced by our mother, in our mother tongue that we hear while sucking at her breast; it's much later, when weaned off our mother's milk, that we turn our heads to listen to the outside world – the world of our fathers. While there is no such expression as 'father tongue', the notion of fatherland becomes very much part of our consciousness. As toddlers, we begin to converse with our closest ones in a childish prattle incomprehensible to outsiders. We then grow into having a private voice with the local accent of our family clan, as well as the one we learn to use in public, in which this or that private accent is only partially suppressed. We are forever doomed, it seems, to be bilingual in the broadest sense of the word, nourishing our mother tongue in private and, simultaneously, adapting our speech to the common usage and accent accepted among our compatriots, in our fatherland.

Advocates of multiculturalism say that our 'private accent' should be cherished and encouraged. Perhaps. There is an opinion, indeed, and not entirely baseless, that foreigners who speak without a trace of foreign accent are most probably either spies or professional tricksters. But our family-given tribal accent, as well as a foreign accent, exists only in the ears of a listener. Being on one's own, the person doesn't detect, doesn't hear any accent – family's or foreign.

When we are on our own and communicate with ourselves – with what is known as our inner voice – we speak without any sound, as it were. You can think of it as our soul's voice. Our inner voice, our soul speaks with no accent. In any religion of the world, God hears your inner voice and does not judge you by your nationality. According to the Bible, God – believe it or not – creates individuals, not nations.

We want people to hear our accentless inner voice, not our garbled foreign incarnation of it. But how to reproduce our inner voice – a voice in our head – that has no perceptible identity? Authors achieve this task through their writings. The simple truth is that this mysterious undefinable inner voice of an author is just the narrator's voice of this author's book one opens to read. And if the book is the one you like, the one that captivates you entirely – whether it is fiction or nonfiction – it fuses its author's personal and national identities, ethnic origin and social background in a fashion that transforms the author: from one who was a stranger with an exotic accent into a confidant – making a direct way to the reader's heart.

Some Thoughts on Foreignness

MICHAEL EDWARDS

Though well used now to writing poetry and prose in two languages, I still come to French and to English with a sense of discovery. They are always *more* than one thought, as are the worlds they name and offer.

I am 'between' languages in that I translate occasionally from several languages into French and from French and other languages into English. I am mostly conscious, however, of being 'in' two languages, day by day, moment by moment.

The strangeness of a foreign language: the whole of reality sounds different, its rhythms have changed, another syntax has articulated it in a way unsuspected before. A foreign language presents itself as a complete system. Its speakers seem to utter it with the perfect ease of the unfallen Adam and Eve. It comes to one as a poem.

The expression 'the gift of language' takes on a new meaning. All those worlds offered by the thousands of languages that surround us.

As well as presenting another world, a foreign language presents a different idea of what language *is*. All the workings of French suggest that language is seen by its speakers as sited in its own world above reality so as to observe, understand and raise it into the scholarly intelligible. (Think of *empreintes digitales* as opposed to finger-prints, or *un hebdomadaire* rather than a weekly.) English exists in the successiveness of time, of events, in the close gripping of the real, even when engaging with the most elevated thought. Though both descriptions are no doubt only partly exact.

French resembles an intricate helicopter hovering over the landscape to survey it, English a deep lane leading one, under a tall sky, through the turnings of the countryside.

I live quite a bit in Latin and Greek, and am glad not to know them so well that they would seem natural. I still find my mind forever adjusting itself as I follow the not-yet-simplified and strangely satisfying word order, which rearranges the world and makes it continually surprising.

When speaking a foreign language, even mouth movements change. The world in that language emerges not only for the mind but for the mouth, the ears, the eyes in reading, the whole body as rhythm. One knows this new world as one knows the world one comes from.

As with the initiation into a foreign language, the first words we meet in life are sounds, strange and full of magic. It's good if all words remain so.

Mouth movements: even when reading in any language with lips closed, I'm aware that the mouth is following the words. When reading literary works this seems even more important, as a miming of their sound. I even prefer returning to the ancient habit of making the mouth movements fully, visibly – though I reserve this for when I'm alone!

A foreign language is firstly new sounds and music, new rhythms, new syntax, and then a world emerging. But, to my knowledge, the beauty and the implications of the newness are not taught to language learners, and the emerging world is rarely analysed and compared.

A foreign language is good for you. And it takes you out of yourself.

In French I've invented the word *étrangèreté*, a noun combining *étranger* and *étrangeté*, 'foreign' and 'strangeness', so as to describe a non-native language as both foreign – in a way, alien – and alluringly, absorbingly, strange. It can also indicate what is beyond the fine but limited rational world in which the dominant strain in European thought invites us to confine ourselves.

The amazement created by a foreign language turns one's own language into a source of amazement, as one considers it from elsewhere. Even a poet, who is forever being startled by the language he has always known (probably the initial cause of his being a poet), can find new reasons for wonder, new things to explore.

Reality speaks to us in our native tongue. For the English, the world is full of events occurring in a continuous present (the baby is being bathed), of things relating to each other in the articulation of prepositions and adverbs ('up through', 'out from under'), of phenomena clothed in insistent consonants ('Of man's first disobedience... Brought death...'), and so on. A great moment in one's progress into a foreign language is when it too becomes the language of reality, the language which, whatever one considers, is what one spontaneously hears.

Yes, but as we know, it's also the case that in another light, equally true, words and things separate. The babelic names for a tree, *arbre*, *Baum*, *dendron*... fall from it like dead leaves. Even 'tree' alone, considered by an English speaker, can be stricken by meaninglessness. Why 'tree'? We are both at home in a creation of which we are a part and prevented from entering it in the goodness of its origin. To go back a few generations, words 'slip, slide, perish', 'Things fall apart'.

A single word concentrated on at length becomes either a marvellous something dense with strangeness, or appalling nonsense. Why?

We must get beyond Saussure, not leaving him behind, since much of what he says still rings true, but thinking as users and not theorists of language. He finds his place in a larger whole when we take into account the feel of words in our memories, and the even longer memories in words themselves. Adventuring into another language makes clear the arbitrariness of words; *living* two languages – or one – reveals their stored-up truth.

The otherness also of a foreign language, I find, rebounds on English. English becomes other, a linguistic structure which, though continually changing, is complete in itself, as opposed to me and my world, and is a cosmos of sound which seems to animate, to transform even, whatever it enters.

One's *langue maternelle*, the language of one's mother, becomes strange.

There is foreignness, as one knows, inside English, a Germanic language peppered with Latin. A fortunate, undisturbing foreignness.

The hybrid nature of English gives one access to the imaginative realities of both the Germanic and the Latin worlds, to which, at different levels, one belongs. One only needs to become conscious of this to find those rich worlds speaking in one's words.

The movements which, from time to time, seek to avoid Latinate words in favour of the 'true' English language developed from Anglo-Saxon are clearly misguided: following them would diminish the resources and the rich taste of English. Though Sir John Cheke's 'gainrising' for 'resurrection' does feel movingly right.

Dealing with French day by day makes me even more aware that the English vocabulary and English ways of placing us in the world that are derived from Anglo-Saxon do seem, when compared to anything derived from Latin, more real and more *ours*. Even *otherness* is somehow more solid – and closer to home! – than *alterity*. Poets, of course, know this, as they know the power of Anglo-Saxon monosyllables ('Why this is Hell, nor am I out of it', 'Be still, and know that I am God'...).

'Profound' tells one that something is deep. 'Deep' takes one there. Two perspectives, both true. And 'profound', though ultimately from Latin, can have an Anglo-Saxon ring and reality, partly from its closeness to 'bound', 'hound', 'pound', 'round', 'sound' in their Old-English derivations.

The extra pleasure of moving specifically between English and French (rather than English and German, English and Chinese) comes from their being polar opposites, at once very alike and extremely different.

The distance between English and French is clearly shown in a comparison of the opening lines of *Paradise Lost* and Chateaubriand's (prose) translation. Used in teaching either French in England or English in France, the comparison would be illuminating and deeply beneficial.

Writing on, say, La Fontaine or Sartre in English, and English poetry (*Le Génie de la poésie anglaise*) or Shakespeare (extravagantly, five books) in French has been a bizarre and enjoyable experience. I don't know whether or not I present an English view of Racine, and I'm quite certain that I don't have a French view of Shakespeare, but hearing any writer through commentary in a language not his own does create an interesting puzzlement, and adds to the pleasure.

The foreignness, the otherness one meets in a language not one's own encourages the perception of further othernesses. In the poet, for instance. As poets know by experience, a poem is always written by someone other than one's self as one (probably mis-) knows it: words call up words, phrases flash in from nowhere, cadences come, the best ideas are often unexpected.

A foreign language, by causing one's own language to appear foreign, confirms that one is oneself foreign to oneself. A Christian doesn't need the theories of psychoanalysis to tell him; he knows the infinitely ungraspable Pauline teaching about the 'old man' and the 'new man', about 'not I but Christ' living in one.

Learning other languages taught me (as did, later, *Genesis* Chapter 2) that language is firstly a way of naming the world and of relating to it, of existing in it. Watching my children and grandchildren living their first words, and the return of childhood in my poems, remind me of this obvious fact, which is forgotten in talk of language as essentially communication.

For the child, the poet, for anyone prepared to listen carefully to a living language, to words as living, it's not even enough to say that a word is a name we give to something: a word is what the something (be it object, action, feeling, relationship...) seems to say to us. Who knows what Adam heard, saw, felt when naming the animals?

From Gainsborough to Constable the trees of England, along with their surroundings, changed. As did French trees and places when Cézanne and Pissarro painted the same scene, their easels a few metres apart. Like painting, like all the arts, literature changes the world as perceived, from writer to writer and from country to country. To write is to watch a new world emerging. The simplest sentence spoken effects a change. I imagine this is well known, but how easy to forget it. Or not to reflect on what it implies.

Each language is another world, but, as with all the paintings of trees or all the poems about love, the world is still there, reality still speaks and waits. The change, rather than sending one into the wilderness of post-modern relativity, prompts one to ask *why* such change, and to wonder what real change would be. In moving from one language to another one need not lose one's bearings, and one can think hard about newness.

Poetry, as all the arts, changes the world in our perception of it. A poem in English and another in French change it in quite different ways. A Christian can understand this newness, and the desire that leads to it, as the ineffectual yearning for Eden and as the glimpse, through a glass, darkly, of the 'new heavens' and, more particularly, the 'new earth'.

Translation also changes: seen positively, into something new, seen negatively, into something impoverished. A fine translation operates rather like the musical setting of a poem: as a welcome transposition.

I don't relish reading translations of works that I can read in the original. But the Bible in German, say, makes the text come differently alive. The authors seem to be speaking in tongues. And one must suppose that the intention behind the Bible, and beyond its authors, was strangely that it *be* translated.

Rather than translating my poems between English and French, French and English, I re-write them as if I were beginning them afresh in the other tongue. Composing the bi-lingual collection *Rivage mobile* confirmed (for me) the rightness of this approach.

I think I understand the fear of the foreign, the sense of loss when forced into using an unchosen language, and the desperate need to return home. But I've been lucky to like and to admire French, to have felt it as part of my experience since an early and long immersion in Racine – chosen because of the kind of foreign intimacy I had with him from the start – and since re-discovering myself through falling in love with a French woman.

I miss England, now and then, while knowing that I can return when I like, and while doing so on occasion. From here – from Paris or from Burgundy – England is a memory, a lost paradise (warts and all) that appears, at times, as a fiction I may visit at will. It resembles Spenser's 'lond of Faery', the real England which emerges through Spenser's poetry and narration and in which Queen Elizabeth really has her 'realmes'.

The pleasure of returning to English! – in reading and especially in writing. The variety and adaptability of the language, its openness to the foreign, its delight in accepting words from other languages along with their un-English pronunciation and even with diacritics alien to English: *coup d'état, tête-à-tête...* English suddenly feels like a giant, generous, true-speaking poem.

Writing *poetry* in French may be the ultimate test ('It can't be done'); it's also a great, instructive pleasure.

I've written several bilingual poems, so as to explore the different ways of looking through English and French eyes, and hence the different things I want to say, and the almost opposing resources available to say them. Here is a sample, a poem, like the others, untranslatable as far as English and French are concerned. It's taken from my book *Paris aubaine*:

L'Agoraphile du Trocadéro
'Dans ces murs voués aux merveilles'

A golden girl in a cape
Nourrit sur son cœur un pigeon d'or ;

The ruffled grisaille of another paddles at her feet
Dans le peu profond d'une eau de pluie.

Les colonnes de pierre et de verre se répondent
In muted echoes within the grand

Hauteur sous plafond of the wide, alluring site
Une Chinoise libérée, flush with poses,

Aims to amaze by the termless variety
De son être intime qui se multiplie en sourires.

*

Breathless, the myopic visitors observe
L'écran mémorieux de leurs boîtes magiques.

A turret room glitters with windows, an eyrie
Pour l'envol des mots précaires du poète.

En haut d'un immeuble, des cyprès filiformes,
Alert Giacomettis, are tense with looking.

The touchwood mind alights on the least
Feature, the smallest scruple of the scape.

Le regard s'apaise dans les lignes fraîches
Des chemins, des terrasses, du bassin.

*

A backward glance from below to the terrasse wall
Discerne les touristes en brèves statues.

Six pigeons sur un arbre sans feuilles que le ciel
  dessine
Search by their shuffling how best to embellish it.

In the wings of three ducks a throbbing motor
Anime les airs et sonde le silence.

Words in the clouds, shape-changing, fleecy,
Tombent en métaphores inventées par les vents.

L'âme délassée habite ce rectangle de buis
That folds a parcel of nature into an open box.

*

Au-dessus du jardin, deux avions de concert
Sign the sky with Saint Andrew's cross.

Quietly the walls of the city have been pushed
  back;
La pensée traverse les murs perméables de l'air.

A soundless wren ignores my unsafeness.
Le soleil, comme la mort, me regarde fixement.

Tu essaies de lire les volumes de la voûte,
A swinging door to the signalling stars.

Il suffit de s'asseoir et de n'attendre rien
To feel the world waiting, like an empty bench.

Creating Ancient Languages

ANDREW BISWELL

Anthony Burgess's enthusiasm for making an artificial language is well known to readers of *A Clockwork Orange* (1962), in which the first-person narrator, Alex, speaks an invented teenage idiolect with elements of Russian, Romany and Cockney rhyming slang. For a later novel, *M/F* (1971), Burgess devised a Romance language to be spoken and sung by the inhabitants of a fictional island named Castita. Another slang, built according to similar principles, is devised by members of the underground university in his novella *1985* (published in 1978), this time based on elements of Hindi. All of these linguistic games have their roots in the pan-Eurish language of *Finnegans Wake*, often acknowledged by Burgess as one of his favourite novels, and chosen by him, when he appeared on *Desert Island Discs*, as the book with which he wanted to be stranded.

Jean-Jacques Annaud's *Quest for Fire* (French title: *La Guerre du feu*), one of the most original films of the 1980s, is set 80,000 years ago. Based on a French novel by the Rosny brothers, the film dramatizes a conflict between the Ulam, a group of hunter-gatherers, and their deadly rivals the Kzamm, a tribe of cannibals. The Ulam have not yet discovered how to make fire, but a lightning strike provides them with a flame which they keep burning until it is extinguished during a raid by the Kzamm. Naoh, a young Ulam (played by Everett McGill), goes on a long journey to meet another community, the Ivaka, and he is taught how to make fire by Iva (played by Rae Dawn Chong). There is no dialogue in French or English: the only words spoken in the film are in Ulam, Kzamm and Ivaka.

The languages invented by Burgess for *Quest for Fire* are not as well known as they deserve to be. One reason for this is because the film contains no subtitles: the challenge for the viewer is to learn the unfamiliar languages spoken by the main characters by ear alone. Another reason is that some of the work undertaken by Burgess did not survive into the final cut of the film. The 'Ulam Dictionary' compiled by Burgess is considerably more extensive than viewers of the film might have imagined.

A range of materials which document the creation of 'Ulam', the main language spoken in the film, have survived in the Burgess archives located at the Harry Ransom Center in Austin, Texas, and at the Anthony Burgess Foundation in Manchester. The commission from Annaud was to make a speculative reconstruction of proto-Indo-European, thought to be the ancestor of modern European languages, which does not survive in a written form.

Although Burgess was originally asked to devise two languages of no fewer than sixty words, the final version of Ulam runs to more than 160 words. It seems that he was excited by the opportunity to develop a complex language, and he delivered more than he had been paid for.

The surviving papers indicate that the Ulam dictionary went through at least three major revisions, and that Burgess's languages were constructed and revised over a period of around ten months. Burgess began his research by consulting some of the books he had studied as an undergraduate student at Manchester University in the 1930s. He relied quite heavily on the account of the evolution of Indo-European languages given by Otto Jespersen in his book *Growth and Structure of the English Language*, published in Leipzig in 1930.

Burgess also consulted his collection of 'Teach Yourself' language books which are now part of the Foundation's book collection. The surviving volumes document his wide-ranging study of modern languages such as Dutch, Gaelic, Greek, Hungarian, Icelandic, Persian, Portuguese, Spanish and Turkish.

When it came to constructing the 'new' languages for *Quest for Fire*, Burgess, drawing on a variety of linguistic roots, combined elements from Indian, Armenian, Hellenic, Albanian, Italic, Balto-Slavic, Celtic and Germanic languages. He paid special attention to Sanskrit, on the basis that this was 'the oldest surviving language of the Indo-European group', and because T.S. Eliot had included a handful of Sanskrit words in *The Waste Land*. Burgess's various engagements with Eliot's poem include a long commentary essay, reprinted in *The Ink Trade*, a volume of his selected journalism (published by Carcanet in 2018) and a complete musical setting of the text for narrator, soprano and chamber ensemble.

His method of language construction was based on the traditional comparative philology he had been taught as a student. Looking at the word for 'father' in various modern languages, he found 'vater' in German and Dutch, 'pater' in Latin, 'pitar' in Sansrkit and 'faðir' in Old Norse. Working from these examples, he concluded that the Indo-European word for father 'must have begun with a lip-sound, the middle consonant must have been dental or alveolar, and there must have been a terminal r-sound'. Following these principles, Burgess decided that the Ulam word for 'foot' would be 'powd' (as in the French 'pied' or 'pedes' in Latin). Water would be 'aga', with the same word used for 'river'. 'Dondra', derived from the Greek 'dendron', is the Ulam word for 'tree'. Fire itself is 'atra', related to the English word 'hearth'.

Speaking about his constructed languages in the 1981 television documentary *Quest for Fire: Behind the Scenes*, Burgess said: 'What I think language sounded like then was a perpetual babble. We have been taught to think by the *Tarzan* films that primitive man used grunts. It was not like that at all. Probably man developed language in order to cope with situations when visual gestures were no use.'

Words are only part of the sign-system known as 'Ulam'. The other significant element is a series of gestures to accompany spoken words, developed in collaboration with the anthropologist Desmond Morris, author of *The Naked Ape* and *Bodytalk: The Meaning of Human Gestures*. In the final version of the Ulam dictionary, dated 30 May 1980, physical actions are indicated alongside the words to which they refer. To communicate aggression, there are three different forms of sound and action. Mild aggression is indicated by repetition of 'Tka, tka, tka', with a side-to-side swaying motion. Moderate aggression involves the word 'Dga, dga, dga', with more vocalisation and resonance, and with increased body movement. The strongest and most violent form of aggression is communicated with the words 'Arr', 'Ang' and 'Arm', with the mouth open, the voice coming from the chest, the lips pulled back to expose the teeth, and a dominant stance.

In 'Firetalk', an essay about the development of his invented languages, Burgess gives examples of how the basic linguistic units of Ulam can be combined to form utterances. Offering a sample Ulam sentence, he cites the following from the film: 'Oyoon itjon s dondron s tsed tirdondron s dondrsitji tsedon'. This translates into modern English as 'We will go into the forest and kill deer with our darts'. Burgess provides the following notes: '*Dondr*: tree. *Tir*: animal. *On*: plural suffix. *Oyo*: I. *Itj*: go. *Tsed*: kill. *Sitji*: diminutive suffix. *S*: invariable preposition conjunction.'

Annaud maintained that Ulam was very useful as a tool for communication. Throughout the long process of shooting the film in Iceland, Canada, Scotland and on the shores of Lake Magdi in Kenya, the director found that his multinational cast and crew, who did not share a common language, fell into the habit of using words from the Ulam dictionary in preference to French or English.

Reading the complete dictionary gives us a fuller picture of how Burgess thought prehistoric people might have used language. The film dramatizes his vocabulary and gives the words a shape, combining J.H. Rosny's novel, Gerard Brach's screenplay and Annaud's visual imagination.

Quest for Fire wasn't the only occasion when Burgess attempted to devise an ancient-sounding language resembling Indo-European. Asked to adapt *Oedipus the King* by Sophocles for the Tyrone Guthrie Theater in Minneapolis in 1972, he added a series of invented-language chants, which were scored by the composer Stanley Silverman for voices and instruments including shawms, a bull-roarer and 'ancient drums'.

The chorus performs the first of these chants as a prologue to the action while a human sacrifice is taking place on stage. Burgess and Silverman decided that no translation should appear in the programme, the point being that the words and music should create an atmosphere of intense strangeness. This interlude is sung or chanted by the chorus before the second act:

> Regwos leikwasti / The darkness goes
> Soite soite / Sing it sing it
> Stere Stene leikwasti / The barren thunder has left
> Soite soite / Sing it sing it
>
> Sneudhos puitur / The cloud rots away
> Pure albhowe behlo / In the bright white fire
> Regwos dheuit / Darkness dies

When it came to publishing the book version of *Oedipus the King*, Burgess insisted that his Indo-European chants should be omitted, on the grounds that 'they only work auditorily and must not be chewed over by captious scholars'. The quotation above has been reconstructed from Silverman's handwritten score and a copy of the rehearsal script marked up by Michael Langham, who directed the first production in Minneapolis.

Given the presence of six substantial Burgess archives in Canada, the United States, France and the United Kingdom, there are plenty of opportunities for further research into the circumstances in which he devised fictional languages, as well as the origins of particular words. Burgess's work in this area turns out to have been more prolific than most commentators have assumed. His approach to linguistics was arguably more creative than scholarly, but there is no doubt that it was motivated by genuine and well-informed curiosity about the pre-history of modern languages. On the evidence of his published and unpublished work, Burgess emerges as one of the few novelists who created a complete set of secondary worlds with internally consistent languages. Above all, he wanted them to be intelligible, memorable and useful.

Lost Languages

PHILIP TERRY

I was born in Belfast, Northern Ireland, where the official language was, and still is, English. I never heard anybody speaking Gaelic as a child, and I didn't know of its existence until, many years later, I read the novels of Flann O'Brien (one of the many pen names of Brian O'Nolan), among them *The Poor Mouth* (1973), translated by Patrick C. Power from the Gaelic *An Béal Bocht* (1941), which originally appeared under an invented Irish pseudonym which O'Nolan used for his *Irish Times* column, Myles na gCopaleen. And yet, the language of Northern Ireland as I experienced it growing up wasn't quite monoglot: there were those who said 'shit' and those who said 'shite', those who said 'bread' and those who said 'pan', those who said 'little' and those who said 'wee'. There was, in a word, an 'official' English (English-English) and an 'unofficial' English (Irish-English). And this was also reflected in pronunciation. My grandmother, who came from York, and who spoke what I always regarded as a slightly affected English, would constantly berate us for saying 'fork' pronouncing the 'r' ('*forek*'). 'There's no 'r' in it', she'd say, 'It's "*fawk*"'. To which we'd reply, laughing, 'There's no "w" in it granny!' Like many of my peers I was, for a brief period, sent to elocution lessons to iron out this aberrational pronunciation – I still remember some of the exercises like 'red leather, yellow leather, red leather, yellow leather' which were designed to improve our pronunciation. But they didn't work – they just became a source of laughter and struck us as ridiculous, and I soon quit these lessons, without anybody making much of a fuss as far as I can remember.

At the same time, growing up, I was in many ways surrounded by different languages, as my father worked in the Spanish Department at Queens University, and I'd hear Spanish, Portuguese and French spoken on a daily basis, and once, when some stern external examiners from Iceland were put up at my parents' house one summer, Icelandic. I wasn't much of a linguist, and language didn't feature on the curriculum in my primary school, but I learned to say a few sentences in French ('Je suis un elephant') and Spanish ('¿Cuánto cuestan las cartas de juego?'), and I enjoyed even more making up Spanish-sounding nonsense words like 'escarapañelo', as well as inventing nicknames for myself and my closest friends – I went by the name of 'Mole' (pronounced 'Moley'), my best friend, Emma, was called 'Bike' (pronounced 'Bickey'). I'd forgotten all this until I started writing this piece, but I think this enjoyment in 'making up' and 'making', which came through playing with language, was one of my first real pleasures, and it's something I found too in junk modelling, my favourite activity at school, which to my mind has much in common with making poetry. I'd link this too to the joy I experienced in made-up worlds, such as the Angria of Charlotte and Branwell Brontë, which I came across in the tiny books in the Brontë Parsonage on holiday in Yorkshire, and I remember in this connection spending long hours inventing a world inhabited by bacteria with my friend Andy White, which we drew on endless rolls of tracing paper into the wee hours.

When I moved to England in the early 1970s, I quickly had my Irish accent and my Irish-English flattened out by the demands of RP – at school in Colchester I was made to feel 'shite' whenever I said 'shite', and I learned to conform to survive. Here English schools triumphed where elocution lessons had failed. But later, much later, when I belatedly became interested in reading, and then writing, many of the interests that had been planted in me while in Belfast began to resurface in one way or another. I found myself drawn to writers such as Camus, Robbe-Grillet and Beckett, whose work seemed not to describe the *world-as-it-is*, like the realist novelists of the English tradition, but whose worlds seemed to unfold word by word, sentence by sentence, making something new as they did so. And I was drawn too by those writers who seemed to invent new languages to tell their stories, such as Russell Hoban in *Riddley Walker*, Anthony Burgess in *A Clockwork Orange* and Joyce in *Finnegans Wake*. Beckett's *Watt*, in this connection, was an eye-opener, with its punning language, circling away from and returning to the name Watt. And in Seamus Heaney, whom my parents had known at Queens, I found a writer who revelled in his Irish-English, bringing to poetry words like 'buckrakes', 'haycocks', 'pebble-dashed' and 'catspiss', with the bravura of a young Baudelaire. Later still, I started to learn French, picking up where I'd left off in Belfast, and spent some time teaching in France, at the Université de Caen, where I picked up a book about the Oulipo in FNAC. I found their ideas immediately engaging, the lipogram reminding me of some deranged elocution lesson, and the idea of constraint struck a chord. Ever since I'd had my accent beaten out of me I'd found something constraining about the English language, and here was a way to engage directly with this idea of the constraining and turn it on its head – counterintuitively, for Oulipo, constraint becomes the springboard for creativity. Ever since, my writing has engaged with Oulipo in one way or another. In the novel *tapestry* I combined some ideas from Oulipo – most obviously the idea of conjuring tales out of marginal images in the Bayeux Tapestry in the way Italo Calvino conjures stories out of the tarot pack in *The Castle of Crossed Destinies* – with the invention of a language, creating a 'lost' English that might have been spoken between the end of Anglo-Saxon and the beginnings of Middle English: 'Weeks and weeks of incessant dull regn, which falls off the sky lyk cow piss. We haue nefer seen the lyks of it. So heavy it es that the watter-tracks boorst theyr banks spillyng ofer into the fields and mice run vertically up the trunks of trees to take refuge on the branches, where they hang in theyr hundreds, lyk strange unsaisonable fruit.' In *Quennets* I made use of and adapted Raymond Queneau's poetic form of the elementary morality. In *The Lascaux Notebooks*, whose word grids owe something to Oulipo's idea of 'combinatorial literature', I didn't so much invent a language, as imagine that the cave signs in the caves at Lascaux could be interpreted *as a language*, as the first hidden and encoded traces of Ice Age poetry. And in *Dante's Inferno* and *Dante's Purgatorio* I used a method of Harry Mathews from his *Trial Impressions* which he calls 'up-to-date' to 'translate' Dante across time and place to modern-day Essex – in something of the manner used in Heaney's 'A Riverbank Field' from his collection *Human Chain*, where he translates from *Aeneid* Book VI, shifting Virgil's topography to rural Ireland:

> Ask me to translate what Loeb gives as
> 'In a retired vale... a sequestered grove'
> And I'll confound Lethe in Moyola
>
> By coming through Back Park down from Grove Hill
> Across Long Rigs on to the riverbank –
> Which way, by happy chance, will take me past
>
> The *domos placidas*, 'those perfect homes'
> Of Upper Broagh. Moths then on evening water
> It would have to be, not bees in sunlight...

One of the curious things that happened to me in writing *Dante's Inferno* and *Dante's Purgatorio* was that I found myself being returned to a language world that was hybrid, like the world of 'official' and 'unofficial' English I had been brought up in – the book, partly influenced by Dante's own use of vernacular, partly by the New York School, employed both standard English and unofficial Englishes, slang words and Irish-English words. And this in turn connects to the way the book indirectly drew me to write about Ireland. When I came to work my way through Dante – substituting Ted Berrigan, one-time visiting professor of poetry at the University of Essex, for Virgil, substituting the river Colne for the Phlegethon, and so on – I came to see that Dante's Florence, which had exiled him on pain of death, would have to be replaced by Belfast, my own home town. In *Dante's Inferno* Ugolino became Bobby Sands, and in *Dante's Purgatorio* Ireland came to take centre stage. In Canto XIV Dante discourses on the river Arno, getting some anti-Tuscan feelings off his chest. I took the occasion to write about the Lagan, and some of the doleful places it passes on its route to the sea, including the Maze Prison. Here we encounter two representatives of the Dublin fashion scene, and elsewhere we meet George Clancy, murdered by the Black and Tans in his home in Grange, County Limerick, and Archbishop Connell, Primate of Ireland, embroiled in the sexual abuse scandals in the Catholic Church. In Canto XVI, which takes place in clouds of smoke in Dante, and here takes place in clouds of tear gas, the pilgrims encounter raised voices heatedly discussing the peace process, and talk as they walk to Martin McGuinness. We encounter Samuel Beckett, Sean O'Casey, J.M. Synge, and in the closing cantos Shane MacGowan is brought back from Hell on an Arts Council 'exceptional talent' scheme to do a gig on the earthly paradise at the top of the mount of Purgatory.

As well as this cast of characters from Irish history, I found my imagination returning to places I'd known in my childhood – Drumbeg, where we used to go mossing, Tollymore, Slieve Donard, Skellig Michael – and the poem too draws many of its similes from Ireland. I'd wanted to write about Ireland for many years, but something, perhaps distance, perhaps my feeling, like that of many Irish relocated to mainland Britian, that I no longer felt fully Irish, had prevented me from doing so. Working through Dante unleashed my imagination, which through this indirect approach was able to fully engage with Ireland, both in its history and in its present. It's something I can't quite explain, but it is in the spirit of Dante, that subjects only come to life if approached obliquely. Dante himself, in the *Inferno*, wants to make the direct approach, hiking straight up the mountain of Purgatory towards his goal, but he is chased back by wild beasts, and can only proceed by taking the circuitous and winding tracks that lead him spiralling thorough hell.

Another innovation in Dante is the way the *Comedy* is filled with both famous characters – popes and writers and kings – and people only Dante knew. In a word, he makes use of what is at hand, what surrounds him, and I found myself doing the same thing, putting politicians like Boris Johnson in the poem, but also a few people, like PhD students (Tony Tackling, my Belacqua, is one of them), that would be recognised only by me and a few others. This method is a lot like the junk modelling that I mentioned earlier, and it's one of the other ways that the poem returns to the milieu of my childhood Belfast, here in the very method of the writing. What I'd call my 'languages' of Belfast – the different Englishes, the making of worlds, the techniques of junk modelling – all make a return in the making of *Dante's Inferno* and *Dante's Purgatorio* in a word. And this marks a return, on one level, to lost languages, the languages that were partially erased when I first moved to England. This theme of lost languages, hidden or suppressed voices, is one that forms the theme of much of my writing, I now see – it's there most obviously in *tapestry*, which tries to resurrect the hidden and unspoken stories behind the Norman conquest in an invented language of its own. And while it is a story set in the distant past, it's also one which connects to and translates my own name, Philip Terry. Philip ('lover of horses') links to the Norman destriers that enabled William the Conqueror to triumph in the Battle of Hastings, and which are everywhere in the Bayeux Tapestry, while one translation of 'Terry', a name of French origin, is 'terre isle', or 'earth island', like the mountains of earth that the Normans threw up (the 'mottes') for the construction of their castles. Lost languages also form the starting point of the unravelling of Ice Age signs in *The Lascaux Notebooks*. I was forcibly reminded of this in what was for me a rare, if not unique, epiphany, which occurred during the composition of this book. I was in the caves of *Les Colombelles* near the village of Les-Eyzies in France, researching paleolithic art for *The Lascuax Notebooks* (another work of indirection, ascribed as it is to the invented poet Jean-Luc Champerret), when a drop of water fell on my head. The guide laughed, and said that that drop of water, from the moment it fell as rain, would have taken fifty years to work its way through the limestone layers above the cave before it fell on my unsuspecting head. And then I realised that the raindrop must have fallen in my childhood, when I was living in Belfast, and still spoke with a Belfast accent, long before I moved to England, and had that accent forced out of me by taunts and bullying at school. And as I realised this, I realised too that my long search for a way in which to write, which had now taken me deep into the earth, perhaps had its origin in this partial extinction of my voice round about the age of thirteen. It was later the same day that I had a revelation that was key to unlocking the poetry that went on to form *The Lascaux Notebooks* – I suddenly realised that the three-by-three grids that were to be found in Lascaux could be filled with signs found in the cave, and that these grids, once filled with signs, might then be deciphered to make poetry.

Double-Think

KIRSTY GUNN

Someone came to look after us. How slowly I printed out the letters. *S...* for *Some..one. S...* for stranger. And how strange I had become to myself that day. The capital letter, I remember, had to rise to the ceiling of the first line, yes, and be perfect. It was the first letter at the top of the panel of six ruled lines directly underneath the part left blank for where I was to make a drawing afterwards. And that *S?* It was for a *Someone* I couldn't yet name, a word of such uncertainty and doubt it felt as though it was barely a word at all. The middle part of the *S* had to curve in the centre of itself and curl back again to sit neatly on the base of the line. 'A perfect little snake' is what our teacher called it – and she might as well have been talking about me. For at the moment of forming the first letter of the sentence I would write, I was in the act of becoming one myself. *Sssssss...* I could hear it. Snake in the grass. *Sssssss...* For secrets. *Sssssss...* For lies. For thinking one thing, and writing another. For *Someone came to look after us.* I finished the sentence. It was done. I was five years old and I had committed my first infidelity to language.

This is the earliest instance I can recall of being formally aware of there being, within one vocabulary, two registers of speech. That there existed in my writing and reading world two very different ways of reflecting experience: a this and a that, a right and a wrong. The teacher had asked us, as she did every Monday morning, to write a story about what we'd done in the weekend. This was a composition as well as a handwriting class – and, yes, that snaky *S* had to be neat and tidy but the real effort of the exercise came from the work I had to put into masking the betrayal I was committing to one kind of language by choosing another. For that 'Someone', my mother's mother, was a word that hid behind it the tumble and confusion of the sort of sentences and phrases, pronunciations and rhythms and syntax that abounded on that New Zealand side of my family, and could not, must not, be released within the stapled papers of my composition book. All those rural elisions and softened consonants, the casual arrangement of nouns and adjectives that should have been adverbs or carried verbs, or the sentences missing verbs altogether: 'You good, honey?' 'You fresh with that bath?' Along with rounds of expletives: 'Jesus Wept!' and 'Take your damn own time', and the unmanageably intimate, gentle affections, the 'honey's and the 'darlin's we never heard at home... I had silenced the lot by sending a 'someone' onto my page instead who would never speak that way. Who was only a someone else instead. It was as though, in one morning's lesson of primary two, I had come to own the complexity of my Scottish and New Zealand inheritance of language and the way the former dominated the latter to such an extent that I could only recognise it – now that I was actually confronting it through piece of writing I myself was making – as a form of speech that had to be corrected.

For: Good English. Clarity of intention. Grammatical sense. How these concepts dominated my education and understanding of one's means of expression and thought. And yet, how the flip version of all that propriety popped up like a-jack-in-the-box – the many phrases and words that the 'someone' contained and that were so different from the way our family spoke – in the musically, forcefully forthcoming speech and manner of my maternal grandmother. Who wasn't even a grandmother, was she? Not a 'Granny' as my Scottish grandmother was? Nor a Grandma or Grandmother as all the other children had? No, she was 'Nanna' – and with the word (the country cousins called her, even more complicatedly, 'Nan') came all the power and surge of thinking about and being a different kind of person altogether. One who existed not only in another part of the country but in an equally distant grammar, with a set of linguistic priorities that were at far, far remove from the only other 'Nanna' I knew of who was in 'Peter Pan' – and she was a dog. And how could I get all that down? All that questioning, doubting, uncertainty, in a composition class on a rainy Monday morning in winter in Wellington, in New Zealand, in the mid-sixties? I couldn't. The 'Someone' was all I could manage.

They lived in the rural centre of the North Island, the family on our mother's 'side' (a word our father repeated as though to remind us all through our upbringing of what side we children were really on – i.e. the Scottish side, the proper side, the authentic and grown-up and responsible and cultured and intelligent side – all inferred by comparison to my mother's wild and volatile relations made up of rural, farming stock with their calling voices and maddeningly intimately informal syntax. Theirs was a way of life and interpretation of the world come straight out of a place of wide skies and big sheep stations, of small towns with 'Milk Bars' and 'Main Streets' and shops known by the Christian name of the proprietor. So: 'Go up Nelly's for six fruit buns...', 'My magazine from Jim...', and 'N-half doz'n' – (it sounded like that, prepositions and connectives and vowels missing on all fronts) 'apples from Chan's'... All contributing, these kinds of instructions and sets of words – none of which would be spoken, and spoken in that kind of way, in the house where I grew up – to a form of language fitted, as much as the land and its people and grasses and waters, to the orders and rhythms of the seasons of the southern hemisphere and its vast Pacific light.[1]

The house where I grew up was a house of clipped sentence endings, using the right words, forming proper phrases, clear vowels and syntax and no swearing except by my father when he was in one his tempers. We had Scottish words for all the New Zealand things so they weren't New Zealand things at all: 'burn' for creek, 'coast' for beach, 'dinner' for tea – and so it went on. We didn't know a single Māori person nor knew the proper Māori words for the trees and flowers that grew there. Yes, we saw tuis, but we drew robins, or put them in our stories – though my mother's mother's best friend was a Māori woman and Nanna spoke often of the plants in her garden with those other names and used words like 'pa' and 'tangi' and 'kai', along with the word 'eh' that softened sentences and seemed to make of life a casual and relaxed affair. Her sentences, and those of her friends, sounded adrift in time and open to New Zealand experience in a way the writing and speaking at school or at home couldn't seem to allow, and which I forgot about until I came to read the wondrously hand-made prose – for that is how it seemed! A kind of writing made up to suit its purposes exactly, not forced for one second from any Western literary tradition or canon – of the Māori fiction writer Patricia Grace, as well as the work of the poet James K. Baxter, with his *Autumn Testament*, and then more. That distinctive New Zealand kind of English language – Grace's discrete shortened sentences and fragmentary dialogue, the Māori inflections and rhythms and words, blended into one, malleable whole – the syntax of a country open to its own temperatures and emotions, its languors and possibilities, of sitting in the kitchen for endless-seeming mornings drinking tea and smoking cigarettes, 'having a yarn'... It was a world away from 'I beg your pardon' and 'Excuse me' and 'Can you please tell me that again?'

I'd never had a moment's hesitation in composition class before. I loved it. Loved writing the neat and tidy little story of what I'd been doing on the weekend, making the sentences lead towards the ending, choosing the words. I loved forming the letters as neatly as I could – using for guidance the three pale blue lines that kept the small letters below the middle line and allowed the capital to rise up to the top. I loved every second of the whole process, the thinking and the writing and then making the drawing to illustrate the story afterwards.

But that morning: I sat for long minutes, powerless and silent, before I could pick up my pencil. My mind couldn't find the words. I couldn't write 'My grandmother came to look after me' because that was not who Nanna was and the words for such a grandmother wouldn't fit nor describe the experience of the weekend at all. Yet neither could a 'Nanna' be made to live within the ruled grid of the exercise book. A 'Nanna', that word, and everything it stood for... It would have to be freighted into another story I hadn't been brought up or schooled in to imagine or represent or think about or understand.

So I wrote, so I spoke – for I had to read the story aloud to the class after writing, we all did – so I betrayed. And that was only a small part of the redaction and eradication of a kind of language – a rich and supple and mobile and highly subjective, ever changing, often very funny and sweet, and infinitely gentle form of expression – that I used to hear on the country holidays of my childhood in the rural North Island of New Zealand but was as though it didn't exist back in Wellington where I was born, with its Scottish school and church and ceilidhs and piping recitals and Highland Balls. And how very strange – my own peculiar form of 'Caledonian Antisyzygy', to paraphrase Edwin Muir[2] – that my father's 'talk', from his 'side' of the family after all, would become, when we lived so very far away from the Scotland we called 'home', my dominant language, my single speech. Though, here I am thinking about this now, and about Edwin Muir's essay and more, and it is perhaps no wonder.

After my mother's death, when I was older but still young, my father announced that 'that's it' – that there was no need to see any of that 'side' of the family again. He'd adored my mother but it wasn't his pain of losing her that had made him pronounce the end of her story. No. It was the language of her family – their speaking and so, therefore, their way of being – he wanted to finally root out once and for all from his so-called 'Scottish' children's speech. 'No need for any more of that sort of thing now', he said, or something of that sort, and that side of life was closed off, pretty

1 See 'There's Always Song in the Water', by Gregory O'Brien, a book flooded with the waters and light of Pacific New Zealand, and a poetic call to inscribe its seas and tides as part of its land's map.

2 See *Scott and Scotland: The Predicament of the Scottish Writer* by Edwin Muir, a book that makes sense of 'double-think', of double writing, of the relationship of poetry to prose – and more.

much, altogether. I didn't hear it again, as actual words sounding in the present tense of the air around me, until I was on a beach in Auckland, many, many years later, with my first daughter as a baby who had been hospitalised upon our arrival in New Zealand but was now on the mend and healthy again. There was a big Māori family having lunch on the sand, and an older woman looked over at me where I was with Millie at the water's edge, and I caught her eye. 'My daughter has been very sick,' I explained to the woman 'and I'm just so relieved she's better.' 'Ah...', the woman smiled, a big smile, 'You got your little girl back again, eh?' she said. 'That's good...' And I could have wept at the sound, with the recognition of it, of the lost language, of her voice.

(M)other Tongue

ANDREW McNEILLIE

Were I ever to be asked to name my native language, say in a form-filling context, I could only say English. The form's an entirely functional device. It simplifies matters and that's what 'the authorities' like. Their statisticians are not interested in nuances or caveats of any kind. 'My' and 'native' and 'language' go unexamined. So does the matter of *when*. I had a native language once. It came in a form of English that entered my ears from the mouths of parents, one of whom (my mother) was a Londoner by birth (but somewhere of Welsh extraction, her maiden name being Hoyles, a very old Welsh name), the other a mix of Scottish birth and Irish origin. I prefer the term 'mother tongue' to native language. The mother is the infant whisperer, the original shaper.

Though how far that carries anyone along is an open question, dependent on social circumstances and cultural exposures. Maybe too the distant echoings from the wireless of BBC 'received pronunciation' played a part, or indeed of 'Workers' Playtime', while my language acquisition gates were still sufficiently open in the second half of the 1940s. Who can say? Welsh was not spoken in our home. But surely the voices of Welsh neighbours, and in the schoolyard, conditioned my ear beyond doubt, as did hours of daily hymn-singing, much of it in Welsh, in post-war North Wales.

All this meant I was well primed (as *PNR* readers might know already) to discover the poetry and other writings of Dylan Thomas around and about when I was sixteen. Thomas didn't speak Welsh. His Welsh-speaking father refused to allow it in the house. What was his native language? His mother tongue was Welsh but his mother was forbidden to speak it at home. His accent was rather grandly English, in patrician BBC style with added *hwyl* in the Welsh pulpit fashion. The effect of my encounter with Thomas's poetry is still a living presence for me. But so is the effect of other early and slightly later poetic encounters. One quite early such exposure I value especially highly was with Anglo-Saxon poetry, another with Gerard Manley Hopkins, and with Wilfred Owen, not to mention W.B. Yeats, Louis MacNeice or 'J. Alfred Prufrock' or, even, 'Hugh Selwyn Mauberley'. And so on. If there is a line to draw under it, it's impossible to draw it, and it wouldn't be a straight one, something more like a flourish, though horizontal rather than vertical, of Corporal Trim's walking stick as in *Tristram Shandy*. But horizontal of course as to line-endings and the work of one step forward, one step back rhyme.

Since my teens, far from my nativity, my English has evolved, studied at a famous university in England, become more sophisticated, acquired a vocabulary and syntax of reasonable range and versatility. These were things I wasn't born with, or into, ranges and rhythms I didn't get at my mother's knee. So add it all up and here are my facts: English is not the native language of Wales (nor strictly is Welsh – it wasn't born there), English is not my native language, English is my mother tongue, but my mother soon ceased to have any linguistic influence on me. I have been told that my father's voice (the writer known as Ian Niall) resonates in every word I write or tale I utter. I think that is probably close to true. Give me the benefit of your *craic* he used to say to me, tell me the story of your life, when I was a boy. He still inflects my voice and syntax.

When we first attempt to utter we speak burbling nonsenses or we wail our hearts out. This should remind us that language is founded as uttered then articulated sound as well as sense, and poets would say inextricably from sense. Or so they *should* say of a matter that has been the case down the centuries all the way to Homer, who was blind. Language is also accent. What sense is there in accent, beyond inarticulate geography, national identity, social register? What is or was my native accent or the tenor of my founding voice or, as they are now, voices – for I am a chameleon? There is no discernible original in the organic cocktail that passes for my mind. I can't offer you an answer. I can only leave you with a question, which to my mind is always far better. Don't you think?

Though when I return to Wales my accent shifts and I soon sound as if I've never been away. I pass for a local, without thinking about it. I'm not speaking my 'mother tongue' or with my 'mother accent' on those occasions. But I'm defaulting to a pitch written into me, as if, but not, into my DNA. I'm defaulting to something that wants to tell others, I belong with you. Perhaps this springs from an insecurity. But that's a rabbit-hole too far. I am a native of Y Gogledd (North Wales). I am what the Liverpudlians call a 'Gog' and nor are Liverpool's vowel sounds, especially that of 'o', far from my tongue, because North Wales has absorbed something of Liverpool in its demotic accent, and vice versa.

Languages are born on the move. They are like hunter gatherers. When they settle they risk dying. They must grow, they must forage, they must expand, they must consolidate. They will compete with other language settlers. They are in league with power and the economics of power. (Some scholarly linguist has declared, 'A language is a dialect with a navy', or I'd say, more clearly, a dialect with a legion.) Languages wax and wane like the moon. They are Heraclitean. They are organic. 'All things are a flowing, / Sage Heracleitus says', as Ezra Pound put it. They will thieve and hijack and oppress in the name of an imperium. They besiege and impoverish their neighbour languages and forbid their being spoken, even on pain of death. They infiltrate their neighbours' territory and undermine their economies and law-making. Or they survive invasions, such as the Norman conquest, absorb and rearrange their capital, and their capitol.

Mere orality will not do. Languages need to be written down, to be reminded of themselves and how they'd got to the stage they've reached. But efforts to fix them are doomed. They will be slowed in their course, dammed by dictionaries (blessed by etymologies), such as Dr Johnson's vital holding operation, and then that of James Murray's OED. Soon they overflow the reservoir. Dictionaries must work hard to keep up. Always there will be voices between generations deploring demotic and 'ungrammatical' usage or semantic change. Always there'll be voices declaring, as Pound also put it in 'Hugh Selwyn Mauberley', 'a tawdry cheapness / Shall reign throughout our days'.

When I was young, it was commonplace to be told that Greek and Latin are dead languages. It helped cheese-paring policy makers, led by the nose by statisticians, to edge them off the curriculum. If ever any policy was barbaric and socially unjust that one was. Ask them in fifth-century Athens. Ask me, who was never taught either but one of them for five minutes. But those big languages did not die, they only faded away, to be reabsorbed, as the language of the Roman Empire mutated into the Romance languages. Ignorance doesn't die, nor sad to say does it fade away. Ignorance ignores what's inconvenient or uneconomical to acknowledge, or is 'blissfully' unaware of the whole business, being too hard-pressed to survive, to subsist, in the lee of a literate world.

But this strikes me as too close to mere elementary textbook stuff, and some of it I am sure too sweeping. I can see learned and other eyebrows being raised in Hungary and Finland, in parts of Africa, and in the Indian sub-continent, indeed, as Dr Johnson said, in 'The Vanity of Human Wishes', from China to Peru. However, whether you are a Welshwoman or a Chinawoman, a Welshman or a Chinaman, what can't be denied is that the English language is a wonder of the world, and its literatures, rich beyond words, their range and reach and interconnections without equal. See for exuberant evidence the works of James Joyce whose mother tongue was also English, if of the inimical Irish strain. And English, if you insist, is my mother tongue, my only functioning language, at least as spoken in parts of the island of Britain and, more universally, written.

Now let's move on and put all thought of the pink official form aside, the one on which the clerk (in American pronunciation) declared in capital letters: 'I DO NOT LIKE MY WORK' in W.H. Auden's poem 'The Fall of Rome'. So Auden's 'native accent' if not his language mutated, in small but telling particulars of sound. Clerk and work, I recall at once, are also rhymed by W.B. Yeats in his poem 'Galway Races', though how he said 'clerk' I don't know but I suspect it wasn't as American Auden did. There's nothing more germane here than the idea of the fall of Rome. Joseph Brodsky, writing on Derek Walcott, in 'The Sound of the Tide', had a challenging take on it:

> Because civilizations are finite, in the life of each of them comes a moment when centers cease to hold. What keeps them at such times from disintegration is not legions but languages. Such was the case with Rome, and before that, with Hellenic Greece. The job of holding at such times is done by the men from the provinces, from the outskirts. Contrary to popular belief, the outskirts are not where the world ends – they are precisely where it unravels.

*

Spanish (A Squib)
for Angus Macmillan

Two Lewismen meet up
in a café, in Castle Douglas,
for a little small-language conversation
to comfort their souls.

Four Gallovidian ladies nearby,
exercising their big mouths
in Scots English, overhear
and are puzzled by the foreign talk.

Until, after listening hard,
one solves the problem
and, in a loud whisper:
'Spanish...' she explains.

What is Spanish to some is, I suppose, Dutch to others. If there is a deeper irony here, it is one all but lost in the mists of time. The town of Castle Douglas is in what was the ancient kingdom of Galloway. Galloway is the only southerly part of Scotland ever to be Gaelic speaking, and in its heyday was a possession of the Lords of the Isles. So its people were once much closer to those of the Isle of Lewis than to the population of Scots-speaking Scotland, Scots being in origin, don't forget, a Germanic language close to Middle English. Galloway is also the region from which I derive my Y-chromosome which in turn, together with some Viking, maps back to a specific location in the Glens of Antrim.

What is my nation? as Fluellen enquired. Perhaps he should have asked, what is my language? What is native to me? All I might say is that biologically or zoologically (to nod at Hugh MacDiarmid's 'Drunk Man') no one derives more completely from the islands of Britain and Ireland than I do. But I live in the here and now. English is my mother tongue and I am a monoglot, not to stretch a point. I'd love to think there are monoglot Welsh-speakers but I have never met one. I once jumped a wall into a cliff-top field on Inis Mór, in the days when I was young enough to jump walls, and took both myself and an islandman working there by surprise. He had almost no English. I had less Irish. We could only smile and laugh at each other. I have to say I thought it then and think it still a most desirable state of affairs, a starting point.

Here is the rub. The time comes, at the outskirts, when the mother tongue of the hearth and heart must cede ground. In the case of the unnameable archipelago of Britain and Ireland, it must open the door to English (nowadays the airwaves, the bandwidths, are already wide open), to earn a living, or to further other forms of ambition. It is a plate tectonic interface, with attendant shockwaves. Dylan Thomas could have been bilingual. He might have had the option to be a Welsh-language writer. At least he would have been made to choose between his mother tongue and the other tongue. But he was denied the opportunity. R.S. Thomas taught himself Welsh to heal his wound but not having learnt it by osmosis at his mother's knee could not write poetry in the language of his heart's desire, only prose. So such matters are determined, with notable exceptions. Bilingualism doesn't guarantee choice.

'Native speakers', as the term has it, on the Isle of Lewis, or elsewhere in Brodsky's outskirts, almost certainly will become bilingual as they leave childhood behind, if not before. In a sense they'll become split personalities, for whom a tête-à-tête speaking 'Spanish' in a Galloway café may become a lifeline woven from melancholy and sorrow as much as love. Unlike monoglots, if they are writers, choice is *possible* for those who are bilingual. It carries no guarantee, but then no attempt at writing anything comes with a guarantee of any kind of hearing, or publication, and reading.

Sorley MacLean's decision to write in his mother tongue was a visionary strategy, profoundly political. He created an immortal bulwark against the *beurla* (Gaelic for 'English') that has been deeply enabling for the Gaelic-speaking world, for younger Gaelic-language poets. Iain Crichton Smith (another Carcanet author) could work both sides of the street quite brilliantly. George Campbell Hay, a linguistic genius, could write poetry in almost any language you care to name, but it is his Gaelic poetry that makes all the difference at the outskirts, in the language wars. Hugh MacDiarmid (ditto) hoped to draw Scots and Gaelic into a companion tradition. In the end he fell into the arms of James Joyce's linguistic chaosmos. It's the richer way to go and depends as much on the 'small' language traditions as the 'big', e.g. as the professor says, under the headline: LOST CAUSES, NOBLE MARQUESS MENTIONED, in the 'Aeolus', 'The Newspaper Office' section of *Ulysses*:

> We were always loyal to lost causes, the professor said. Success for us is the death of the intellect and of the imagination. We were never loyal to the successful. We serve them. I teach the blatant Latin language. I speak the tongue of a race the acme of whose mentality is the maxim: time is money. Material domination. *Dominus!* Lord! Where is the spirituality? Lord Jesus! Lord Salisbury. A sofa in a westend club. But the Greek!

This has all been about spirituality and the want of it, in one measure or another, and ignorance. Whatever our mother tongue, whenever and wherever the battlelines are drawn, languages are the *other* that work to make sense of us, and of our nonsense, through the course of time. Pass me back the form will you? I need to write FUCK YOU across it.

Civil readings

IAIN BAMFORTH

A final roar

On hearing someone quote Ludwig Wittgenstein's well-known observation (in *Philosophical Investigations*) that 'if a lion could speak, we would not understand him', the eccentric gambler and zoo-owner John Aspinall responded: 'He hasn't spent long enough with lions'.

The oral type

I once suggested, for polemical reasons, that Friedrich Nietzsche wasn't entirely the good European he thought he was because he knew little about European languages and cultures other than the classical ones (which he knew very well indeed) and the France of his epoch. He once declined to translate Giacomo Leopardi, claiming that his knowledge of Italian wasn't up to it and adding, with a charming false modesty, that in any case German posed him enough problems. It may be the case however that the undeniable rhythm and poise of his German prose style came from a deliberate *restriction* of his interests.

He was also an intensive rather than extensive reader, preferring (against the newspaper-fuelled trend of his time) to concentrate on a few master texts and, even then, to hear them read out loud, in the old-fashioned way. The German, he complained, 'does not read aloud; he does not read for the ear, but only with his eyes'. Reading and listening were quite different activities; and he complained that inappropriate standards were applied to Greek history 'from which alas only the words for readers have come down to us'.

Owing to his poor eyesight, Nietzsche was naturally drawn to the memorable: to short, pithy, rhythmic assertions that came to him on his walks and which he committed to memory, and only subsequently to his notebooks. His failing eyes led him to invest, in 1882, in a prototype typewriter, a Malling-Hansen writing ball. It is a purchase which offers a wry comment on his campaign against the medicinal tincture of the written word, and the Platonic concepts that emerge thereof – as *side effects*.

Not look away

You cannot regard horrors without being tainted by them. Anthony Hecht makes this point bluntly in his long poem 'Rites and Ceremonies' about the persecution of Europe's Jews: 'The contemplation of horror is not edifying, / Neither does it strengthen the soul'. Three centuries before him, Andreas Gryphius concluded his famous poem about the Thirty Years War – after listing all the cruelties visited on the German-speaking lands – with the concluding regret that what tormented him most was not that so much had been destroyed but that so many souls had been 'spoiled by war'.

Amassed

Leopardi in his *Zibaldone* (3508) writes that Dante, 'who succeeds in filling us with fear of the Inferno is not able, even poetically, to give us the wish to enter Paradiso'. With its vision of Heaven alone, he writes, Christianity would not have had the influence that it has. What would we, as distinct ego-beings, be seeking there exactly?

It is doubtful whether in an age of individualism (itself the unfolding of a Christian idea), the divestiture of the body in paradise in favour of some kind of ultimate 'transfiguration' in which personhood is merged into a collective state of blessedness exerts any kind of attraction. Insofar as something as horrific as the Nazi camps encroached on the theological, it was in this negative reappraisal of selfhood: Jews were first stripped of their social identity and ascribed a communal identity (as 'the Jew' or 'Muselmann' or walking corpses who were candidates for immediate destruction in the death camps – Levi calls such a person 'the man who has seen the Gorgon'), prior to their being destroyed indifferently, in a blind mass of bodies.

There is an eerie reminder of this in Dan Jacobson's book of remembrance, a book moreover about the very *lack* of what is remembered, *Heshel's Kingdom*. It relates what its author finds of the nearly effaced record of the war against Jews, the meaning of which is itself an emptiness. Shlomo, his guide around the despoiled villages of Lithuania, almost entirely void now of their Jewish population, and whose distracted attentiveness Jacobson likens to that of 'deaf persons listening for sounds they will never hear', takes the author to one nameless site after the other, each of which he calls a 'mass massacre'.

Shlomo's way of insisting on the words makes it apparent to Jacobson that 'he firmly believed "mass" and "massacre" to be organically connected to one another, through a common root'.

Autopsy

Clearly, an odd talent for laying bare. When narratives, explanations, accounts are cut short, then even the most inconsequential sentence can have a mysterious effect. And there is no predicting how its cadence will float – or rather will it fall? Will it be moralising? Will it be cutting? Will it be to extend a hand, like Keats's spectral one? Or will it be merely strange? But the point is to get through people's defences, including one's own, and touch the raw tissue. 'Here and there we catch a curiously significant phrase and we would almost like to leap to our feet.' (Kafka)

World line

Bruce Sterling, one of the founders of the SF cyberpunk movement, has claimed credit for the neologism 'spime', a contraction of 'space-time'. He uses it to designate a futuristic master object that can be tracked throughout its life span from its virtual representation in the design stage, through manufacture, ownership, physical location until eventual obsolescence and recycling.

This sounds like something that might stir the heart of a product researcher or archivist – a kind of data set cataloguing all possible interactions from object conception to extinction – but there is another, earlier citation for 'spime': it is attributed to Einstein's more speculative notion of 'space-time'. Although some philosophers of science consider Einstein's assuming time to be a dimension and putting it on an equal footing with three-dimensional space a philosophical error, treating it empirically as a dimension has proved to be very fruitful in theoretical physics, and the theory holds up with experimental data. According to Lee Smolin it was a great insight on Einstein's part to realise 'that time is created by the relationships of the changes that happen in the universe, and nothing else. The grammatical distinction between past, present, and future falls apart.'

Curiously enough, one person keen to use Einstein's 'spime' was Ivan Illich, who mentions it twice in his *In the Vineyard of the Text*, perhaps his most appealing book, a history of the twelfth-century theologian Hugh of St Victor's teachings on the art of reading (*ars legendi*), the first of its kind, and on the scholarly habits and fantasies engendered by the fantastically simple technological template we call the alphabet. Illich's understanding of 'spime' would therefore appear to register a new awareness of grammatical distinctions rather than their falling apart as in Smolin's comment.

How to read the Spanish novel

Let me see if I've understood it: Don Quixote dies when he becomes conscious of the real world. Unfortunately, in becoming ethically serious he loses his comic appeal, so that when he dies, the *reader* is obliged to face the sad spectacle of his own situation.

Exile on the Ringstrasse

As Adam Phillips suggests in one of his clearer moments, Freud's work can be seen as a rewriting of his personal history, and psychoanalysis as an allegory of acculturation and his not always successful assimilation as a Jew in Vienna. The child then is the immigrant, who has a home but needs to find a way of living among other people's social arrangements. He is liable to be questioned by the authorities (his parents) and even brutalised; others will always speak for him, knowing better; and the child will go into hiding, not only from those significant others but also from himself.

A refiguration

Cicero and Quintilian remind us that the art of memory, from the very first, has a forensic quality to it. The poet Simonides of Ceos was called upon to deliver a panegyric at a feast to the Thessalian king Skopas, and angered his patron by also praising Castor and Pollux. Called away from the banquet when two strangers at the door (the two dioscuri) demand to see him, the poet turned at the threshold in the split second a commotion started up behind him, only to see the entire hall collapsing, killing all present. He was able to identify the disfigured dead by recalling exactly where they had been seated before the catastrophe.

FA/FO

Sir Richard Turnbull, the UK's last but one commissioner in Aden, told Denis Healey on a visit to the outpost in 1965 as Secretary of State for Defence: 'When the British Empire sank beneath the waves of history... it would leave behind only two monuments: one was the game of Association Football, the other was the expression "Fuck off"'.

As David Bellos writes, 'everything is effable'. Two centuries before, the German philosopher Georg Christoph Lichtenberg, on visiting London, wrote in his notebook that 'If countries were named after the words you first hear when you go there, England would have to be called "Damn It"'.

Intractability

Discrimination is one of those words you can hardly use these days in a positive sense (even though the Americans gave us that curious term 'positive discrimination'). Advanced capitalism's levelling effect on culture – folding it into production – has created the impression that in aesthetics all distinctions can be elided. Yet the act of discriminating or differentiating – marking the differences between things, making a diagnosis – is central to the very idea of a viable culture. Its taint comes from its etymology: it is related to crisis, crime and criteria, all of which stem from the Greek verb *krino*, meaning to judge and distinguish – but also to accuse and condemn a victim. Victim untouchability therefore suggests a new relationship between the collective, the individual and the culture as a whole, which is now much more tolerant, and even indulgent, of those who claim to be discriminated *against*. But that concern for the seemingly victimised is itself a form of discrimination, which simply sends us back to the initial dilemma: it is impossible not to ascribe differences, because every attempt to avoid doing so simply reassembles the differences in a new guise. Wittgenstein surely had this in mind when he told Maurice O'Connor Drury that if his posthumous investigation of language games *Philosophical Investigations* needed a motto, it ought to come from *King Lear*: 'I'll teach you differences'.

Say the name

'The plague (since it must be called by its name)...'. Jean de La Fontaine, in *Animals Sickened by the Plague*, provides testimony to the power of the Word: people do everything to avoid mentioning the dreaded term and thereby unleashing its evil on the community.

Leaflets

The feuilleton was invented in 1800 by the French journalist Julien Louis Geoffrey, an editor at the *Journal des Débats*, who used leftover space in the paper's advertising section to launch his own cultural commentaries: the name persisted even when the feuilleton ('small sheet') was incorporated into the main body of newspapers which imitated his practice. In the nineteenth century, the feuilleton was regarded by nationalistic Germans as decadent and spurious. It was also identified as 'Jewish' and associated with Heine, who was castigated for emigrating to Paris and importing the 'foamy French passion drink'. Another critic was even more forthright about defending the virginal virtues of German culture: 'What the Jews do today is to strip all discipline from thinking, sodomise the word, deflower and feuilletonise the intellect, and turn it into a prostitute in the newspaper and the market hall'. Other attacks on the feuilleton came from high modernists such as Musil and Adorno, who criticised it for false subjectivity: it adopted a personal tone but was in fact formulaic and often prefabricated. Theodor Lessing remarked that 'the word "feuilletonist" is the nastiest insult in the German language'. He made the remark in a 1929 feuilleton.

A Pharisee

Someone who asserts that had he lived in the time of the prophets he wouldn't have ganged up with the others to put them to death. This superiority to events is practically a confession of personal susceptibility to the contagion that leads to prophets being stoned.

Which came first?

Most scholars suggest that Romanticism – and the explosion of imaginative energy in novels, music and painting – was a *reaction* to the massive changes that swept over Britain and then Europe in the late eighteenth century with the Industrial Revolution, but there are indications that a massive change in consciousness *preceded* the revolution in social and working conditions. It has been suggested that the 1740s were the hinge decade. Samuel Richardson published his novel *Pamela: or Virtue Rewarded*, which was very successful and hugely influential – it is often thought of as the first (modern) novel. That same year Adam Smith went to study at Balliol. In 1745, Emmanuel Swedenborg had a vision in a London tavern and believed that he had been appointed to reveal the true meaning of the Scriptures. In 1746, Samuel Johnson – who more than any other figure stands for the continuity between tradition and modernity that has characterised British national life – was commissioned to begin his work on *A Dictionary of the English Language*. Also in 1746, the last pitched battle was fought on British soil, and although the Jacobite cause and the Highland clan system lost the war, Scotland would serve as a major scene for the staged playing out of this intensification of human imagining. In 1747, the concept of 'beaux arts' was established in Paris by Charles Batteux. If the human imagination was not passively reacting or adapting to changed circumstances (i.e. retreating into a daydream free of the oppressive realities of urban life, forced work and blighted surroundings), what was it about the mid-eighteenth century that lent itself to such a dramatic increase in reach and ambition?

William Blake, a follower of Swedenborg in the next generation, even believed that the Last Judgement had taken place in 1757, as described in the master's *The Heavenly Doctrines*, and that the Lord had returned, as promised in the New Testament. Swedenborg was adamant that this 'second advent' was not 'in person', as many literal-minded Christians thought, 'but in the Word'. Humankind was thenceforth living in an entirely new dispensation.

Brute events

'A cry doesn't call – it exults.' So writes Gaston Bachelard in his strange little essay on Lautréamont's *Maldoror*. This is perhaps the same ecstatic scream embraced by Antonin Artaud, defiantly affirming itself in a kind of self-immolation. An expression that can't contain itself, according to Socrates in *Philebus*, where he associated the cacophony of opinions with the sounds of people hollering in the street.

Not the kind of extended totemic exultation Vincent van Gogh heard when he painted, though, or the lucid cruelties Artaud aspired to produce in the theatre – 'outside thought'. Max Ernst wrote of his 1930s' collages, especially *Loplop the Bird Superior*: 'My works from that time were not destined to seduce but to produce howls'.

Nowhere without no

James Wood writes somewhere, commenting on his upbringing in an evangelical Christian household in Durham, that 'once religion has revealed itself to you, you are never free'. His assertion is worth pondering, and not only in relation to his revelation: I have been nursing a similar conviction for close on forty years, having been made to sit in on a similarly (perhaps even more) evangelical childhood in Glasgow, without ever being very sure what the nature of that revelation was. Prayer, enforced prayer, was a big part of that childhood; I can't ever recall joy or adoration, certainly never anything like the moment recounted by Augustine at Ostia, in Book 9 of the *Confessions*.

An earlier generation, perhaps two or three back, experienced this revelation as the absence of God: Martin Heidegger, brought up as a rural Catholic in Swabia, insisted that this absence was 'not nothing' and could even be considered a heritage if seen full square: in the epilogue to *Das Ding*, he wrote that 'the flight of the gods must be lived and endured'. And the problem goes back much further: Coleridge was already struggling to reconcile the discipline of thinking with the ultimate mystery of human relations. This is why French thinkers in the mid-twentieth century – Blanchot, Levinas, Derrida – rephrased the issue of faith: there is no God but I must have faith in the other person talking to me. We are born into a world of relations; none of us is a monad. Words and signs are learned and interpreted by individual minds, but that isn't where they subsist: they flutter in the larger sphere of their communication. The point of knowing them is to be a user of signs in a community of sign-using selves, although we can become selves only when we exchange them with others.

And then there is literature, which as a substitute-faith offers some of the command of the Gospels, but with less authority: a book may possibly be life-changing but is unlikely to be soul-shattering because it lacks the force of the absolute: 'you must change your life'. You can just put it down and walk away. But perhaps the revelation hangs on whether religion derives etymologically from *religare* ('to bind') or *relegere* ('to read again and again'). It is clearly apparent which derivation is more congenial to the literary critic.

Agent provocateur

Henri Godard points out that the simple secret of Céline's success, after his national disgrace in 1945, was to treat the reader not as a fellow sufferer, former companion-in-arms or even person who could be shamed into sympathy by the sorry spectacle of his public disgrace but as an *adversary*. He brought narrative and polemic together in *Féerie pour un autre fois* (*Fable for Another Time*) and discovered that hostility is even more effective than complicity in maintaining interest and attention: it compels the civil reader to wonder what offence he has committed in turning the uncivil author against him. Provocation does what its etymology suggests. In that respect, Céline is something of a literary terrorist.

What remains

An arresting saying from a report (written in execrable English by an Italian anthropologist) on pastoralist groups in the Somali Region of Ethiopia that was my editing task this week, where the men doing the hunting get the prime cuts and the women preparing the food eat what is left from the children's plates: 'Women grow better by eating their husbands' remains'.

A self-confession

All my childhood, I listened, with a slight sense of worry, to my mother talking to herself in the kitchen. The kitchen was always the centre of the house because that was where my mother was. Her conversations with herself sounded like arguments, and I could tell from my own room by the rise and fall of her voice that nobody else was in the kitchen. It was very Jewish, as if she were discussing the Torah. (Now I do the same thing, except I write it down in my diary, and sometimes I wonder if I've been talking to myself my entire life too.) But while my mother was at one in the privacy of what she was saying to herself, oblivious of my overhearing until I startled her by alerting her to it, talking to yourself in a diary is a different matter altogether. I've no idea if my mother was confessing, though what she was saying did sometimes sound urgent. She was suspicious of writing, and would have regarded the need to mark up one's sins as entries in a diary as a kind of self-observing vanity; and in that she wouldn't be entirely wrong. Writing is the recursive spiral that is always liable to vitiate the authentic attempt at self-insight. But then, talking to yourself is a defective kind of talking, or at least a form of talking derivative of a genuine conversation, which requires us to talk to at least one other person.

Wittgenstein observes in *Culture and Value*: 'When you bump against the limits of your own honesty it is as though your thoughts get into a whirlpool, an infinite regress: You can say what you like, it takes you no further.' Saying is not at issue here, but self-presentation: as Rousseau showed, having to live out your own confession merely makes it a further opportunity for vanity. It becomes a performance trick. And that is only one further twist.

Between English

ALEX WONG

Even those of us who are embarrassingly monolingual, at least in the sense that we cannot habitually make ourselves understood in any but one language, may feel suspended between languages. We may put ourselves into that position. And do we ever, in fact, succeed in making ourselves understood in any language? Living in the suspension may be a response to that problem.

In the common sense, and beyond very specific situations, I can communicate effectively in English and no other language. I would be unable to write this essay, to rewrite the contents of this essay, in Italian, French or Latin. But I have at various times tried to improve my reading of these languages, and working through translations of poetry, translating always into English, has been a different kind of 'communication'. It plots one, however punily, within the Republic of Letters and puts one into contact with the literary equivalent of a Communion of Saints.

But into what English? Not into my 'native' English, although I am a native speaker of English. In translation from Latin or Romance languages it is easy enough to import something of the character or structure of the source language into the English, and still easier to play, more or less freely, with etymologies and verbal kinships. I suppose one could do the same with Germanic languages, and that it becomes harder with those less closely related to English. This is of course not most people's idea of 'faithful' translation, the transfer of content with as little fuss as possible; it is not even necessarily a transfer of form, but a mix of transformation with whatever novel elements spring additionally from the confrontation between languages. Often this is what I seem to want: to affect, infect, inflect the English, making a new English – even if only for the present moment or for a single task, although it seems to me that usually the process is not one of discrete utilitarian tasks but of a continual evolution with variegation allowed in. To capture something of the strangeness of the encounter, something of the character of the original language, perhaps something of the character of that language specifically *as* made strange, ephemerally, by juxtaposition with the character and resources of this other language, the receiving one. Many translators do this, in varying degrees.

Could it be that this attitude, or this desire, is particularly appropriate to a person characterised partly by mixture and ambiguity, and not only in ethnicity? Someone who does not feel quite at home in any particular kind of English, although English (in its broadness) becomes a most important home? British and American English – I was moving between these in childhood, and there was mobility of accent as well as of idiom and vocabulary. But then there were also, and more troublingly, the class-marked uses and varieties of British English, an obstacle course in which taboos were clearly in place but poorly understood. I was not allowed to say 'ta'. Many of the things my own extended family said, my immediate family did not wish me to say. My parents' English, like everyone's in some degree, was hedged by taboos and guided by social aspirations and identifications, and yet these identifications were not strong enough, not sufficiently connected with a community or sense of belonging, to make a home. Language was not a space for the play of identifications, imaginative empathies and bondings, but a tool with which to present *(one's) identity*. Let us please retain poetry for the former and not solely for the latter.

The aspirations, too, were not at all connected with a culture in which richness of language and nuance of meaning seemed to be cherished. I had little exposure to literary language, but at the same time my exposure to vibrant, playful speech was policed and modified by anxiety – a class anxiety which was undigestible to me at the time. Where language seemed most vital and expressive, where there was obliquity and nuance not merely for the sake of convenient evasiveness, but for play, and where the play of slang suggested and fostered belonging, there tended also to be trouble. This must happen also with those who grow up speaking a regional dialect distinct from, though considered subordinate to, the official language. Speaking it or hearing it spoken.

So what was my 'native' language? Where had my parents' native languages gone, the ones, if any, in which they felt really at home? (In my mother's case, a kind of English.) Insofar as I had a native language, it was an anxiously impoverished one, cut off both from a putative and repudiated commonness and from the communality of a literary culture. (It is tempting to think of these as poles, but I think that would be wrong.)

I might have been brought up bilingual but was not. Chinese, my father's Cantonese – which in his Malaysian upbringing, with an anglophone schooling, would have been mingled in use with the colonial language and perhaps other Chinese dialects – was not taught or spoken to me. When it was spoken in my presence, it was outside of my immediate household and in a way that did not imply my potential participation. Quite early I had the impression, and may have been told explicitly, that my monolingual mother would not like it if we children and my father were able to communicate in a language unknown to her. Triangles, then, and language as a possible tool for covertness and evasion. I did, however, spend time with a Chinese great-grandmother who had no English whatsoever: an experience of the transcension of profoundly felt alienation, presumably on both sides.

Irish Gaelic was far in the background on the other side: my maternal grandmother, which whom I spent much time in childhood, made references to it and brought out the occasional phrase for my curiosity, but had lost whatever fluency she had once had; and my mother's generation spoke English only. My father's Chinese, too, was probably already becoming patchy after decades in England; and what was the constitution of 'native language' for him, in the poly-lingual environment of British Malaya and new Malaysia?

The two sides of my family, each from a former British colonial territory, had largely left behind their other languages in favour of English. Many years of lessons at school, meanwhile, left me innocent of French but eternally guilty of the lack of it. An attempt to learn Italian, briefly intense at the start of my twenties, was conducted on two fronts, one conversational (i.e. how to interact in a restaurant scene) and the other based on the reading and translation of Petrarch's *rime*: manageable, owing to his relatively narrow range of interests and repeating vocabulary in those poems. In that two-pronged approach is evident already a clear tendency to think in terms of a literary language – historical and yet still relevant and current – as being at one with but differentiated from an everyday language of oral interaction. And I have felt more at home in the Petrarchan language than in the stumbling language of any *caffè* encounter; not being a talented linguist, in the literary language I have been able to spread modest roots of a kind.

And is Petrarch's language living or dead? The language I have engaged with most closely, though with great effort and blundering, has been a dead one, or one whose continued life is almost exclusively confined to the page and not to speech: classical Latin.

When translation from a foreign or dead language is not in question, there remains, then, a related question: that of historical manifestations of English and their status with respect to the present culture. Is the language of Thomas Browne strange enough to be foreign? Is Middle English a dead language? Short of Chattertonian fantasy – (though he brought more poetry out of fake Middle English than out of contemporary verse) – and avoiding, one would hope, the more sentimental fantasy of historical nostalgia and the aureate allure of certain literary trappings, what may a modern writer *do* with archaism, and in fact with all the 'outmoded' resources of a changing language that remains fundamentally itself?

Literary language is always between languages. Literary English is always between Englishes, and, more distantly, between other languages too. In any moment I may pause between, say, Malory and a text message, between Landor and London slang, between George Meredith and Eileen Myles. Strange places to be, but you make a nest or campsite. They are 'in' my native language, the interstices and the paired counterparts that bound and define these, but to me they are hardly native, even most of the slang. I have travelled a way to get there, or just to have the capacity – from moment to moment – to arrive in such places, and this makes an important part of their experiential character. The resulting literary language may incorporate the language I learned in childhood, but the state of being suspended in it seems impossibly far, and starkly different, from the condition of that first language – when it was an 'only' language, even while always expanding and diversifying into context-appropriate subsets. Literary language for me as a monolingual writer does not seem merely an expanded and enriched 'only' language, although the ways in which I write prose inflect, more or less, the ways I think privately and, in some situations, speak. But is it really no more than another sub-language, fit for one more particular context and function? Literature, and an approach to it that sees it as legitimately diverging from, just as it may legitimately converge with, the sort of English (not purely spoken) that one learns as a 'native' tongue, has made a very different experience of the language generally and totally, as well as making for the separation, when it appears, between the literary and non-literary.

The general language, when felt as unified, is then more multiple, more complex, allowing for in-betweenness. Less satisfactorily, one could say that the *two* languages, when felt as distinct, take on the aspects of a narrower 'native' language and a multifarious literary one (which perhaps includes elements of the native Englishes of others). But the perspective gained from the latter allows one to approach the former, too, with a hunger for complexity and expressiveness that directs one into a between-state: the wanting to get between this language, even without importing anything concretely 'literary' or strange. And this, in a sense, brings the native language back into the literary dimension.

Getting between the language: I associate this with Geoffrey Hill's ideal of 'writing *into* the language', which, as I think he explained, implies for him both inscription and something of the sense in which a bird or plane takes off *into* the wind. Such an intervention into the language, as I think of it, gets between itself and itself.

I often remember something Gerard Manley Hopkins wrote in a letter to Robert Bridges. 'The poetical language of an age should be the current language heightened, to any degree heightened and unlike itself.' To any degree! Literary language is kept lively by the tension between naturalness and alienation.

*

After reading the editorial in *PNR* 281, in which Michael (I can't call him Schmidt) described his automatic tendency of reversion, in a Spanish-speaking environment, to the Macaulayesque English prose of his youth, I wrote him an email to remark that I too had experienced (not to say suffered) from the very same influence as a boy. A baleful influence as most would think. But I was pleased by Michael's balanced (or ambivalent) attitude as well as by the coincidence. In the editorial he had written:

> As a boy I loved Macaulay's elaborated sentences, the affectation yet vigour of his syntax, and his abundant vocabulary which wore its etymologies on its sleeve. *The History of England* was my Whiggish bible, and it took many years to recover from it.

I responded, initially trying to rough my prose up a bit:

> Oh, oddly enough Macaulay's 4-vol History of England (which I still have in the same copy) was also a style model for me too in school days. I suppose that won't be much of a surprise... Unlike you, I don't think I ever did recover...

Not quite an apology, in any sense of the word. A specific memory then appeared:

> I remember in history lessons trying to express my thoughts in a Macaulayesque manner. This was often a matter of actual plagiarism, and they weren't my thoughts at all. In particular I recall an essay (aetat. *c.* 12) in which I offered from memory a version of a long sentence of his, which had seemed very elegant, on the topic of Charles I and 'ship money'. I don't believe this was noticed by the teacher, which left me puzzled. Surely he should either have suspected foul play or castigated the ineptly-handled archaism as a folly in itself.
>
> This was quite probably my very earliest experience of thinking, in a very crude way, about literary style. I hadn't thought of that until now.
>
> I've almost taken those books to the charity shop on several occasions, but I feel strangely bound to them, in spite of their ugliness and my embarrassing memories around them...

It may in fact have been in Macaulay that I first experienced the beauty and satisfaction of prose as such, though I was wholly lacking in the wherewithal to process or absorb this as a lesson either in reading or in writing. I could not reflect on it or do anything creative with it.

Years later, perhaps around the age of sixteen, I was puzzled to the point of serious exasperation when I heard it said that *Dracula* was, 'of course', very poorly written. What could that mean? I was preoccupied by this question, feeling I was in the dark about something important that was self-evident to others – like a child trying to understand sex. It may partly have been that, with Macaulay somewhere in the background, my nascent literary sensibility, such as it was, already favoured Victorian syntax over the pseudo-casualness of much contemporary writing, so that Stoker was bound to seem stylish, articulate and fulfilling. Only a year or two later, with the immensely and immediately thrilling discovery of Ruskin and Pater – both perceptive analysts of style as well as great stylists themselves – was 'style' finally revealed, with peeps at possible criteria. It is Pater, incidentally, who, defending eclecticism in fine modern English style, talks so enticingly about the tense and stimulating admixture of 'long, savoursome, Latin words' and 'racy Saxon monosyllables'. What promiscuity. What promise. Things (or something) to get between.

In one sense, then, these adventures took me deeper and deeper into my native language. In another, they took me far from the language I had been brought up with, far from home. What John Bayley calls 'the inevitable solace that right language brings' – a quotation I find in Shirley Hazzard, who for me is one of the most solacing of authors, notwithstanding her terrific acuity – had not been familiar to me in earlier life. Or it was felt only glimpsingly and was not readily appreciated or absorbed. Inarticulacy can be a kind of trauma, not intense but persistent, again like that of sexuality for the child. The two things are not unrelated. The inarticulacy, or dubious articulacy, of adults can be troubling when it seems intentionally to be hiding things behind a veil, to be dodging, fudging and evading. Much of this has to do with sex. And when it doesn't, it has to do with hypocrisy of some kind, or some other taboo. For many of us, language that fudges and dodges continues forever to be a basic source of distress: language full of denials, an emaciated language of smoke and mirrors, barriers, blinds, messages that don't stand up. Language heavy with law but light on lore. Which is also a language not particularly open to play. (So it was, much of the time, in the household language of my childhood, except in the light euphemism-fog in the mild foothills of taboo. Wee-willie-winkie, dinky-doo.)

Enriched, poetic language perhaps becomes a defence. But it is defensiveness of a positive and outgoing kind, creative: it is a productive way of bringing ambiguities, enigmas and the slipperiness of experience within a range that is tolerable, if not quite within masterful control; a means of communing sensuously with ambiguity and slippage, and of doing this in communication, at least potential communication, with others. Although, as Ruskin pointed out in his depressive way – and I have found it to be true – the more carefully and precisely one speaks, the more likely one is to be misunderstood by most people. The alternative, however, is to be understood only imprecisely, which is only an illusion of understanding: the feeling without the reality, without the content. For many of us, that is, without much contentment either.

One could ask whether, in a psychoanalytic perspective (please skip if hostile), the engagement with an enriched, literary language is defensive in the sense of an attempt to come to acceptable terms with the basic traumatic mysteries and taboos of childhood, which, somewhat transformed, persist societally and in variously individual ways throughout adulthood. Fundamentally, that is, with sexuality, as seen in the psychoanalytic perspective; sexuality as mediated through language, which is sexuality as distinct from 'what the rutting stag knows'. Or we could leave aside 'sexuality' and talk about taboo. But if it is defensive, it is, again, not necessarily in a negative sense; getting 'between' the language is not analogous to getting between the parents (as the Cantonese might have done at home), an obstructive defence against those 'oedipal conflicts' which at bottom are only the perennial emotional difficulties of triangles and exclusion. The question arises whether some other kinds of sophisticated language, of a more objectivistic or scientistically definitive kind, may have something of that jealous and demystifying aspect. But literary, poetic language, so far as it preserves, encourages and allows for an appreciation of necessary mystery, ambiguity, ambivalence, for something ungraspable, is a more positive and less anxious thing even while it thrives on fine distinctions. Among its facets is that of a creative playing with jealousy and with the wanting to know about those things in life from which we are excluded. It gets into creative relationship with mystery. I am struck again by the usefulness of the concept of 'negative capability', which of course does not imply a relaxation of the desire for precision or articulacy.

I will come back to Hopkins. *'The poetical language of an age should be the current language heightened, to any degree heightened and unlike itself.'* And to another part of Michael's editorial:

> In the end Philip French, who produced some of my radio work, told me that my style was 'unspeakable' in at least one sense, perhaps two, at which point I began to write a less unnatural, a more sayable English.

Michael, nevertheless, has been importantly supportive of my perhaps unspeakable English. He said to me once that unlike many contemporary poets I 'don't conflate literary language with spoken language', or words to that effect. I took him to mean that I did not assume that the language of poetry had necessarily to be identified closely with natural spoken English of the present day; in other words, that it could be heightened and unlike itself in various ways and to any degree, and also perhaps that it could be so without necessarily going to an extreme of avant-garde disruption of natural syntax. I have found this a valuable permission. While I admire the convincing integration, as thoroughgoing as you like, of natural speech into literary style, I find the pseudo-naturalness of much contemporary writing (especially in prose fiction) a serious obstacle. Somehow it seems more troublingly unnatural and 'literary', often, than a more frankly stylised writing.

Moreover, as some of my reflections above may suggest, the unspeakable English that gets between the English and alienates it from itself is a field in which it is easier to approach the unspeakable. (This time in *at least two* senses.)

The common ideal at present of naturalness of diction makes ridiculous many of the ways in which earlier generations of writers achieved this alienation. For instance, archaism. Spenser could use Chaucer, Keats could use Spenser. The Elizabethanism of the Victorians was practised respectably for decades of the twentieth century. Such gestures are impossible now without thick latherings of irony. Anyone who objects that nothing in this regard is impossible may try it and see how stupid they feel, or are made to feel. And yet, with irony at times a little less than thickly spread, I have risked this ridicule and hoped – though my teaching experience makes me wary – that readers will see play instead of mere out-of-touch pretentiosity. It is often necessary to insist that style cannot simply be read as the assertion of *(one's) identity*, and that the style of a piece of literary writing is neither a claim nor a threat that the writer would actually speak in the same manner down the pub – no more so, and probably less so, than the specialised language we use for an official letter. Maybe, in a general way, stylistic play reasserts mixedness, the multiplicity of identification.

Archaism being a sin, translation or inter-linguistic paraphrase, where I began this essay, offers some excuse for creative estrangement, and (ironism aside) possibly a more viable route, although many readers do not recognize it as such. The kinds of artefact-prizing translation I have described is somewhat analogous to archaism if history is another country. The play of Pound's Propertius, or Canto 1, becomes something of a paradigm. Or the delectable weirdness of Richard Burton's Catullus. Or Browning's bizarre Aeschylus in the *Agamemnon.*

*

When Joachim du Bellay wrote *The Defence and Illustration of the French Language* in 1549, the choice for him was to be between Latin poetry, in which he excelled, and a commitment to the development – the enrichment or 'illustration' – of vernacular French. He encourages the latter as a worthy aim. For 'illustration' he advocates the borrowing and appropriation not only of thoughts but of actual items of vocabulary, suitably modified, from other languages. He aims at 'copiousness' of resource, advising French writers to 'invent', 'adopt' and 'compose' new words out of Greek and Latin. He talks of 'nativeness', of 'something proper to itself alone' in each language, which remains untranslatable; but also of the rewards of freer imitation between languages, a matter of identification, of digestion and of horticulture. The Romans imitated their Greek forebears,

> transforming themselves into them, devouring them; and, after having well digested them, converting them into blood and nourishment, taking for themselves, each according to his nature, and the argument he wished to choose, the best author of whom they observed diligently all the most rare and

exquisite virtues, and these like shoots [...] they grafted and applied to their own tongue.[1]

One may also 'enshrine, like a precious and rare stone, some ancient words' in a modern text, 'usurping' morsels of archaic French from old romances – as Spenser would do in English. They add lustre, illustrate. But the effect may also be of a layering, a mix-up of archaeological strata. Stratification implies the possibility of betweenness.

For Du Bellay, although a native language was 'sucked in with the milk of the nurse', it was precisely because he was looking for a literary language as such, a creation or confection only *based* in natural speech – in other words, because he did not confuse a poetic language with the spoken language but took it for granted that these were to be distinct – that defence and illustration were required. Literary language was to be the spoken French raised above itself and alienated from itself. This is a distinction that cannot be easily made with regard to a dead language, his other medium. Poetic French was to be a peer to poetic Latin. But for Du Bellay's age there was no demotic Latin; records of a more demotic Latin were just as fossilized as the most aureate classicism of Cicero and Virgil, and to modernity still less natural or familiar. French offered this more radical difference within unity, a so much more real differentiation of languages within a single language, where the difference always, in one aspect, would proceed from a fundamental intuitiveness of speech.

What about Montaigne, a strange case, who was raised in a household in which French was forbidden to be uttered in his hearing, and who by his own account learned no French at all before the age of six? Even at school the vernacular would have been used only surreptitiously. He was raised as a 'native' speaker of Latin. He became one of the great writers of the French vernacular. It is usual to assume that the great authors of the Renaissance – the ones now commonly remembered as great, and not the once celebrated Latin writers – gravitated instinctively towards vernacular languages as more vibrant and plastic than dodo Latin; that French was intrinsically richer, more alive, a more stimulating medium and essentially the right choice. Or was it perhaps alterity itself that pulled him to the second language? Something antinomian?

We talk about the 'mother tongue', and there is the 'language learned at mother's knee'. On the other hand, I am reminded in this connection that in Lacanian thought, language is associated with the symbolic, with the law, with the paternal function and the *nom du père*. Latin, in accordance with his father's dictates and proscriptions, was Montaigne's first, and in the common sense his native language. But in what sense native? The cultural continuity to which Latin gave access for the child Montaigne was somewhat abstract, sophisticated, with a long vista. The Latin regime put him out of continuity with most of those really around him, especially most women and most people of the uneducated classes, but also from the educated men and boys for whom Latin occupied a different place in their lives and would not usually have been spoken in leisure, as 'second nature'. Latin was not his mother tongue, not a *langue maternelle*; it was not his mother's language. Neither, of course, was his father, for all his proficiency, a native speaker of Latin. The father, by the way, is extolled frequently in the *Essays*, while his mother, as critics have often noticed, is rather absent from his writings. Montaigne, moreover, tells us that he was sent as a newborn to a humble family in the village near the familial château, nursed by a woman of a different class, among people who cannot have known Latin. This was long before the Latin started. If he sucked in a language with the milk of his nurse, it was French; but an unknown, untaught, unlearned French, to which later he had to return as if for the first time. The Latin must have provided an unusual condition for that return, one for which he might well be grateful. I imagine the nostalgia for something not properly his own, beyond the inescapably literary – and in his case, the legislated – Latin.

I suppose I carry on looking, necessarily within English, for both kinds of continuity: with vibrant, inventive, bond-making speech rooted in day-to-day sociable reality, and with the long vista of a literary culture in which utterance is more or less abstracted from quotidian speech. Play seems indispensable in both cases. I look for these two things in a language that sometimes feels unitary and sometimes divided; and when it seems divided, neither of these languages (for argument's sake to speak of only two) feels entirely native.

But in literary writing these two (or more) divergent languages within the one tongue can be brought *back* together again, although inside the literary domain; brought back together not as if identical, but as parts of a composition.

1 I quote from the translation by Gladys M. Turquet (1939).

Three Poems

MILES BURROWS

Mrs Tanaka's Daughter

I think of her at six years of age
She carries her young brother on her back.
She herds the geese and the turkey in the field.
The turkey, taller than Shao Mei
Advances furiously in the yard
Scarlet wattles engorged with purple rage
Its neck and wings outstretched.
Shao Mei hits it on the head with her bamboo
Not sideswiping
But with an exact vertical swoop
Hits the top of its head.
Stunned, the turkey falls to the ground.
Afterwards, it looks at Shao Mei with respect
And dies.
We often think of Mrs Tanaka's daughter
Small in stature even for that race.
A teenager, she walks home across the graveyard.
In the dusk. A punk on a bicycle
Snatches her satchel. She sprints after him,
Pulls it off and swings it into his face.
– If I'm to be robbed I need a real robber
In a black leather jacket on a Ducati
Not a schoolboy in an old sweater
With drainpipe trousers!
Orphans and foundlings sweeping the temple yard,
We often think of Mrs Tanaka's daughter
And would like to marry her. This is not permitted.
It would disturb the harmony of the eight directions
And would upset Mrs Tanaka.
We often think of Shao Mei as she was then
With her long black hair
Washing her hair in the river at dawn
With Vinolia shampoo
And the monk in his robes running between the trees
In the golden light.
Mrs Tanaka has gone back to her village
How we miss her sharp tongue!
Shao Mei is a high-flying executive
With multinational organisations
Head hunted and cherry picked
With clip board and iphone
She rides a Ducati in a black leather jacket
And has gone to that country from which no traveller returns:
America.
And we are left here in the temple yard
Old men sweeping, or standing in kibu dachi. (The rider's stance)

Uncle Vanya Drinks His Own Poetry

Auntie Biddy could never get the hang of poetry
and was so hopeless that she put other people off.
She was asked to sit outside the classroom and do knitting in the corridor,
which she was happy to do,
but still peered in through the glass pane in the door.
– Poetry? What happened to woodwork?
You can do anything at 70 now.
My solicitor plays tennis with 2 knee replacements.
There are people jogging every morning beneath my window.
They stop when they get round the corner.
They stoop forward as if reaching out in longing for the further shore.
I tried jogging, and a woman said:
– I thought you were a horse coming up behind me.
All that puffing and blowing. Not doing you any good you know!
People write things on walls,
Critics are cleaning ladies with their smiles and buckets.
And used to have names like Harold Nicholson
or Kenneth Clarke, and would tell us what we really liked.
'Glancing again at what we always feel must be an early student of Memlinck
in the little church of Santa Maria della Condolenza,
who is not reminded of that remark by Berenson
that the back view of a woman is, from the point of view of line and mass,
more satisfactory?'
And we think yes of course.
2 women in America are arrested for assaulting a traffic policeman.
(A long loving shot as they are being driven to the courthouse in handcuffs).
This is followed by a wild pony in Alaskan muskeg
that has fallen into a bog
and is waiting to die as its back legs and haunches are being sucked down.
It is pushing up with its front legs
as if trying to heave itself out
Immobile and very young. Big expressive eyes.
Suddenly there arrive two people with a lasso and a belt
like a transmission belt which they manage to fit
round the submerged back end of the pony,
and winch it out gently without breaking its legs.
The pony trots away, with just a brief nod
Like a poet rescued by a small magazine.

At school we were groomed to be well-informed.
The Connoisseur taught us what furniture to appreciate,
What country estates in Radnorshire to acquire.
At least we could become housekeepers,
Agents, or auctioneers.
The kind of people who hold up objects at Christie's
Or lie against the bonnets of slim cars.
We were all spinning round in The Wheel of Fire
Like a cake mix. New York poets.
Stefan was a lecturer in Fashion.
He wrote a poem that began
('The full moon, like an aspirin caught in the throat of a hysterical woman...').

Reading Glasses

Too vain to wear glasses
We go on reading our favourite novel
In its red cloth binding
Like the colour of curtains faded in sunlight
Or the cassock of some retired, perhaps discredited, missionary bishop,
Forgetting the plot which we knew once
And unable to make out the characters' names
'– She wrapped her arm round me like a stole.
It gave her a sense of reliability.
– A sense that was shattered when you made advances
to Mrs Vereagle.
– Advances?
– You were at her like a ferret in a sack sir.'
Unable to remember the plot or read the lines
But remembering we loved the novel
From our favourite novelist
We turn the well-loved pages under the lamplight
So that other characters
With names like Mrs Vershinin
Are always hovering in the wings
Despite the reading light over our shoulder
Like an approaching migraine.
We go on turning the pages
Revisiting a landscape, dazzled by the reading light
Making out vague forms
Strangely altered from faces we knew in childhood
And even changing as we look.
What good value these old novels are!
Who would dream they could be read upside down
And back to front
Like a landscape seen by a child hanging upside down in a tree?

The Sayings of Emma and Eva as Recorded by Their Father

An excerpt

EUGENE OSTASHEVSKY

We live in Berlin. Emma is almost six. Eva is born.

The baby finally has an official name and it's Eva, middle name Livia. Emma, who was ecstatic, suddenly became jealous and asked 'Why does she have two names and I have only one?' She wept bitterly.

25 Nov 2014

'Babushka says she hopes you have a happy birthday tomorrow and get a lot of presents.' 'Did she say how much?'

Babushka = grandmother, Russian.

7 Dec 2014

Emma turns six.

Emma wants to live in a house that is 'so beautiful'. Beautiful in what way? 'It has so much decoration you can't see the house.'

9 Dec 2014

Face painting at a Christmas party. Emma: 'Ich möchte Maria sein! Ich möchte Maria sein!' To Manfredi: 'Magst du Josef sein?' Manfredi: 'Ich möchte ein Tiger sein!'

Ich möchte Maria sein = I want to be Maria, German.
Magst du Josef sein? = Do you want to be Joseph?
Ich möchte ein Tiger sein! = I want to be a tiger.

24 Dec 2014

'Can you stop talking about kaka all the time. All the time, kaka. Stop!' 'But I like it.' 'Why?' 'Because at six you're supposed to do stuff like that!'

7 Feb 2015

Me to Eva: 'Hi, medvezhònok!' Emma: 'What's medvezhonok?' Me: 'You forgot what a medvezhonok is? Baby bear.' Emma: 'Then what's medvezhòn? Big bear?'

(*Medvezhòn* in Russian is a morphologically plausible but inexistent construction.)

7 Feb 2015

'Papa, why do you like privacy when you wash?' 'Because I like privacy when I wash.' 'But *I* don't like privacy when *I* wash.' 'Maybe it's an age thing. Maybe when you're my age, you'll like privacy when you wash.' 'But I don't even like to wash.'

3 Apr 3 2015

'Papa, can you make me a jüdische Stern.' 'Ok, what colour do you want?' 'Yellow.' And she gives me a sheet of purple sparkle paper. 'But with three angles, mit drei Ecke.' Me, frustrated: 'I can't make it with three angles! It's supposed to have six!' Oya jumps in to translate: 'She means make it with three triangles!'

jüdischer Stern = Star of David, German.

3 Apr 2015

Emma: 'I want... I want... I want... I want!' Me: 'What *I* want is for you to realize that happiness can't be obtained by shopping.' Emma: 'Papa, give me a euro.' Me: 'No. Happiness can't be obtained by shopping.' Emma: 'Then give me two euro.'

1 May 2015

Emma: 'Give me thirteen underwears!' Me: 'Why do you need thirteen underwear?' Emma: 'Because I have thirteen bodies... hahahaha!'

15 June 2015

In response to my question before leaving the house, Emma decided to show off her knowledge of Russian and proudly declared 'Ya ne pìsat'!'

Ya ne pìsat' = I not to pee.

28 Jun 2015

'Papa, can I have an afterdish?' 'Do you mean a Nachtisch?' 'Yes.' 'How do we say Nachtisch in English?' 'Afterdish.' 'No. It's a French word.' 'Kwakwakwa.' 'No. It's 'dessert'. Do you know why it's called 'dessert'?' 'Why?' 'Because you have to deserve it.' 'Papa, what's "deserve?"'

5 Jul 2015

'Papa, let's count the steps.' 'Ok. One, two, three, four, five, six, seven, eight, nine, ten, one, two –' A wild howl: 'You confused everything! Now we have to start over again!' 'Why? The second *one* is eleven, the second *two* is twelve... We're now on step fourteen.' 'That's not how I count! You should never count like that around me again!'

6 Jul 2015

I wash Emma's hair. She's screaming and crying. Me: 'Why are you howling?' Emma: 'I am afraid you'll get soap in my eyes!' Me: 'Maybe you want to wait till I get soap in your eyes and howl then?' Emma: 'I don't want to wait!'

25 Jul 2015

At the zoo. 'That's a girl penguin.' 'How do you know that?' 'It has long hair.' 'Emma, that's absurd. Do girl lions have long hair?' 'They can have long hair. They just don't want to.'

1 Aug 2015

'Pee,' suddenly says Emma at lunch, 'is the last number of the number system. Then the number system breaks down... When the number system breaks down, come numbers Kee, Lee, Be, See, Tee.'

13 Aug 2015

Emma starts school.

'Today we apologize for all the stupid things we said and did to other people over the whole last year.' Una: 'I didn't say or do any stupid things!'

(On Yom Kippur, the Jewish Day of Atonement.)

23 Sep 2015

'Come, eat some more.' 'I can't eat any more.' 'If you can't eat any more, that means you can't eat dessert.' 'Papa, you don't know me! You don't know me at all!'

26 Nov 2015

Emma turns seven years old, Eva turns one.

Emma: 'I am the farthest of English-mothertongues... in spellings!'

(Emma's class is divided into native speakers of English and of German.)

12 Jan 2016

So today I get Emma from school early, and she says to me at the kitchen table: 'Papa, is *Unendlich* (= infinite) the biggest number?' I say that there is no biggest number, but that the Infinite is all numbers together. She says, 'Yeah, it's like a different alphabet, not number alphabet, but another number alphabet. The alphabet of *Unendlich*.' Me: 'Did you learn this in school?' Emma: 'No.' (Is this true?) 'I will invent another alphabet, after *Unendlich*', she says. 'The first number will be hundred-thirty, four thousand, ninety.' I write it down: '130, 4000, 90.' (Maybe I should have written down 134, 090, but she said it separately, with pauses). She looks at what I write, then she says, 'The next number will be... two-hundred-forty, five thousand, one hundred.' Then she says (definitely verbatim, I am writing down right as she speaks): 'There is going to be an *Unendlich* that takes the numbers of that alphabet together and then there is going to be a next *Unendlich* that takes all the numbers of the world together, even the biggest, hardest alphabet.'

10 Feb 2016

More on varieties of infinity. This morning Emma asked me to explain 'When the saints go marching in'. I did. Her response: 'But the world doesn't have an end. The world is like a ball. Does a ball have an end?' Then she listed all the boys in kindergarten and first grade who are *definitely* going to hell: 'Felix... Juri... Ramzan...' The way to school was a continuous monologue about her dream of a tornado that 'opened an endless labyrinth to the universe'. The line that struck me: 'The tornado looked just like a hip-hop star.'

11 Feb 2016

Eva's first word. I strap her on my chest to go for a walk and say, 'Eva, schlafen!' Eva, suddenly looking up at me: 'Nein!'

Schlafen = sleep, German.

11 Feb 2016

Me, to Emma: 'What are you saying?' 'Nothing. I am talking my own, um. Language. I am talking my own language.'

13 May 2016

Oya: 'Windel wechseln!' Eva: 'Oh, Mann!'

Windel wechseln = change diaper, German.
Oh, Mann! = Oh, man!

16 June 2016

Emma, on first being told about the Russian Revolution: 'Really? A hundred years and it's *still* a big mess?'

11 Sep 2016

Emma turns eight, Eva turns two.

'Eva, what does the crocodile say?' 'Miaow!'

10 Jan 2017

'You have the hiccups.' Eva: 'Where?'

('Where' probably said in German.)

10 Jan 2017

Studying Russian with Eva. 'Slon. Say slon.' Negative grunt. 'Slon.' Negative grunt. 'Slon.' 'Thlon.' 'Awesome! Slon. Now... Otkuda? Ot verbliùda. Verbliùd, camel.' 'Was heißt Ver...' 'Ver-bliùd, camel.' Eva: 'Wer hat eine blutige Nase?' After shock and jubilation, I take her words down. Then we go back to the book. 'Chto vam nado? What do you need? Was brauchen Sie? Shokolàda. Was heißt shokolad? shoko... shoko... Come, you know what shokolad is. Was braucht der Elefant?' Eva, studying the picture, 'Brille?' Later I catch her walking around the apartment with a pink camel, saying 'Wer hat eine blutige Nase? Das... Kamel heißt. Ka-Mel. Ka-Mel.'

Explanation of the Russian. We were reading 'Telephone' by Korney Chukovsky, a children's poem from 1924. Here is a literal translation, with relevant transliterations:

'My telephone rang. / "Who is speaking?" / "The elephant" (*slon*). / "Where from?" (*otkùda*). / "From camel ['s house]" (*Ot verbliùda*). / "What do you need?" / (*"chto vam nàdo?"*). "Chocolate."'

Explanation of the German. *Was heißt* = What is called, or what is. *Wer hat eine blutige Nase?* = Who has a bloody nose? *Was brauchen Sie?* = What do you need? *Was braucht der Elefant?* = What does the elephant need? *Brille* = glasses.

20 Jan 2017

Now that Eva is beginning to speak English, her negations are all of the *I* + verb + *not* form: 'I want not! I sit not! I go not! I stand not!' (calque of *Ich will nicht*, etc). Not once yet has she used the form 'don't.' But her verbs often remain in German, as does her word order: 'Can you me *erzählen?*' (Can you tell me a story? – Meaning: a story about something I point out or mention).

13 Jun 2017

'Du bist meine Deutschlehrerin!' Eva, indignantly: *'Ich bin* Hello Kitty!'

Du bist meine Deutschlehrerin = You are my German teacher.
Ich bin = I am.

4 July 2017

Reading *Curious George*. 'And the elevator man said: "Just remember, you are here to wash windows!"' Eva: 'No!' Me: 'Then what are you here for'? Eva: *'Gar nichts!'*

Gar nichts = nothing at all, German.

7 July 2017

Sibling rivalry and English pronouns. Me: 'Who's gonna help me pick tomatoes on the balcony?' Emma: 'Me!' Eva: 'No, me!' Me: 'Both of you!' Eva: 'Both of me!'

14 July 2017

'Emma, wash!' 'I washed!' 'There's butter on your face!' 'It's not a lot of butter!'

19 July 2017

Eva keeps saying 'I am a tiger. I am a cat. I am Emmy. I am a bunny. I am Rapunzel. I am Jenny Linsky. I am Elsa', etc. Much of her play and even much of her communication consists in identifying herself in this manner with fictional characters or animals. This must be the identification function of reading – especially with novels like *Madame Bovary* – in embryo.

4 August 2017

'Eva, what's this called?' *'Fahrrad'*. 'But what does Papa call it?' (= what is it in English?) *'Fährrad'*.

Fahrrad = bicycle, German.
Fährrad = 'baecycle', imitation American accent.

27 August 2017

'Emma, let's go outside!' Emma, lying in bed and reading a comic: 'Only if we go shopping.'

10 Sept 2017

Breakfast. Eva, to Oya: 'Nein!' Emma: 'Typische Nein-Phase.' Me: 'Look who's talking! You're still in a typische Nein-phase.' Emma: 'No!'

Typische Nein-Phase = typical 'no!' phase.

24 Oct 2017

Today Eva said 'shes' for 'her'. 'She is combing shes hair.'

2 Nov 2017

Eva turns three years old.

Reading T.S. Eliot's 'The Naming of Cats.' Me: 'Eva, what's a good name for a cat?' Eva: 'Um... Allergy?' (She has allergies.)

13 Nov 2017

Emma turns nine.

Eva: 'Ich bin ein Pferd.' – Me: 'Wie heißt du, Pferd?' – 'Ich heiße Delfina.' – 'Wärest du ein Delfin, könntest du Pferda heissen.' – 'Könnte ich Ferdinand heißen. Ich heiße auch Ferdinand.'

In English: 'I am a horse.' 'What's your name, horse?' 'My name is Dolphina.' 'If you were a dolphin, your name could have been Horsia.' 'My name could have been Ferdinand. My name also is Ferdinand.'

13 Dec 2017

Eva, on the Russian cartoon about the musicians of Bremen: 'It's better than the story of the pig.' Me: 'Huh? What story of the pig?' Eva: 'With Winnie.' (Was all of this in English?)

14 Dec 2017

Eva: 'Ich heiße Punkt, das normale Einhorn.'

'My name is Point, the normal unicorn.'

24 Dec 2017

Eva, on my back: 'Papa, you trag mich... Papa, rennen! Papa, galoppieren!'

trag mich = carry me.
rennen = run.

31 Dec 2017

'Bist du eine Prinzessin oder ein Pferd?' 'Ich bin ein *ganz normales* Einhorn!'

'Are you a princess or a horse?' 'I am a *totally normal* unicorn!'

2 Jan 2018

'No book! I'm spieling with mama!'

spielen = to play, in German.

8 Jan 2018

Eva: 'Papa, warum hast du diese Jacke angezogen? Das deiner Frau gehört.'

'Papa, why did you put on that jacket? It belongs *to your wife.'*

16 Jan 2018

At the entrance. 'Princess, please go up the stairs.' Eva, sitting in her stroller and studying her new unicorn toothbrush: 'Ich habe keine Zeit!'

Ich habe keine Zeit = I have no time.

17 Jan 2018

Emma: 'Papa, I need another cough drop. I am coughing very hard.' 'Silently? Very hard but silently?' Emma, making an effort: 'cough, cough'.

18 Jan 2018

Eva, engrossed in a book, starts scolding, 'Dinosaurier, du musst den anderen Dinosaurier freilassen!' (= Dinosaur, you must let go the other dinosaur!) I once asked Emma at the Natural History Museum, under a black T-Rex skeleton from Denmark: 'Why do you *like* the Tyrannosaurus Rex?' and she said: 'Cause he's so *cute!'*

2 Feb 2018

I am trying to feed Eva shrimps. Me: 'I'm a little shrimpie, swimming in the sea!' Eva, biting: 'Du bist tot, Mann!'

Du bist tot, Mann = you are dead, man.

5 Mar 2018

Kindergarten teacher, in German: 'Eva was tired today and moved very slowly. We are all tired in this weather!' Me, examining Eva: 'Eva has one, two three, four, five boulders in her jacket pockets! Could that be the cause?'

16 Apr 2018

Emma: '... and in the land of Blue Bears everyone has to lie...' Me: 'Why does everyone have to lie in the land of the Blue Bears?' Emma, with a dismissive bah: 'Culture!'

16 Apr 2018

At breakfast Emma let me have it. I did not inflate the pool yesterday and set it up in the courtyard (it was bad weather), I did not do it on Friday either (it was late), I never do what I promise, I am a bad father – and then she ran out of the kitchen, still shouting. Eva and I look at each other. Me: 'She is a tough cookie, your sister'. Eva: 'Cookie?'

3 Jun 2018

Mathis, Emma's guest: 'The Empire State Building is built of around a thousand bricks... no, a million bricks.' Emma: 'It's a billion!' Mathis: 'No, it's a million, a million bricks!' Emma: 'No, it's a billion! I've seen it!'

3 Jun 2018

'Doctor Ostashevsky, help, my foot hurts!' Eva: 'I am not a doctor. I am a pony.'

18 Jun 2018

Eva's English is improving quickly but she still uses German verbs with English pronouns, auxiliaries, ing endings. Last week: 'I'm *spiel*ing' (= playing, from *spielen*). 'I'm *spiel*ing I'm *sterb*ing' (= dying, from *sterben*, said while lying down and covering herself with a blanket). 'I'm *such*ing for the book' (= searching, from *suchen,* maybe used transitively, don't remember), 'No! I'm *mach*ing it myself' (= doing, from *machen*). And 'You try *red*ing *Deutsch mit ihnen*' (from reden, to speak, maybe not 'try', can't exactly recall).

18 Jun 2018

'No zucchini, no dessert.' Emma: 'You are trying to make me eat *everything!* Parents aren't supposed to do that!' 'How do you know what parents are supposed to do?' 'I *know!!!'*

18 Jun 2018

Eva: 'I have not a *Popel*... no, I not!'

Popel = snot.

23 Jun 2018

Eva turns four. Emma turns ten.

'Where did you make peepee?' 'In meine Hose', in my pants. 'No, Eva. *Where* did you make peepee?' 'In meine Hose!' 'No. Where is the *Hose* you made peepee in?' 'Das weiß ich nicht', I don't know.

27 Dec 2018

Eva: 'We're cooking a film.' From *gucken*, pronounced *cooken*, to look at.

27 Dec 2018

Eva: 'Man darf nicht kaka-machen sagen. Man muss 'zitronen' sagen... Ich muss zitronen!'

'You are not supposed to say 'make kaka'. You are supposed to say 'lemonate'... I have to lemonate!'

28 Dec 2018

Darkness. Fireworks. Eva runs towards me. Emma turns to the window and shouts something long, German, and self-righteous, that ends with 'Es ist noch nicht Silvester, Idioten!' (It's not yet New Year's Eve, morons.)

Dec 29, 2018

'There's a New Year's present for *her'* (pointing at Eva) 'but not for me!' 'It's because I told you not to open all your presents early.' 'I didn't *want* to open them!'

31 Dec 2018

Telling Eva about Don Quixote. 'And Sancho had a donkey but I forgot his name. Can you think up a name for Sancho's donkey?' Eva: 'Donkey Hotte?'

4 Jan 2019

Attending supper in a pink ballerina number with princess accoutrements, Eva made gestures at solidarity with the Ancien Régime by musing: 'Die armen Menschen essen nur Kuchen.' Then she broke into 'Für das deutsche Vaterland,' a German anthem of problematic provenance. 'Where did you get that from?' From a book. And then she says, noticing my displeasure: 'Aber du bist auch ein Vater!' but you too are a father! And suddenly smiles.

Die armen Menschen essen nur Kuchen = Poor people eat only cake.
Für das deutsche Vaterland = for the German Fatherland
Aber du bist auch ein Vater! = But you're a father also.

28 March 2019

Me, looking at my phone: 'Oh, it's Lenin's birthday... or is it Hitler's?' Eva: 'Whose birthday?' Me: 'Somebody's but you don't know him.' Eva: 'It's Osterhase's birthday.'

Osterhase = Easter bunny.

22 April 2019

Eva: 'We are going to Edeka or we are gucking Bibi und Tina!' 'Why are you giving me ultimatums?' Enraged: 'I am not a tomato!'

Edeka = a German supermarket.
Bibi und Tina = German cartoon series.

4 Jun 2019

I asked Eva to get herself ready for kindergarten, so she went into the bathroom and put on lipstick.

5 Jun 2019

Me: 'Do you want to ask the kitty-cat her name?' Eva, bending over the cat: 'Meow?' Silence. To me: 'I think it has no idea.'

9 Jul 2019. Izmir

Eva wants attention. Me, with shopping bags: 'If I don't put the food away it will go bad!' 'Otherwise *I* will go bad!'

10 Aug 2019

Emma, smelling a bar of soap: 'Whoever made this soap is a superhero!' Me: 'What do you mean?' Emma: 'It smells epic!'

17 Aug 2019

Oya: 'Papa can play Legos with you.' Eva: 'Forgessiss!!!'
Forgessiss = fugghetaboudit.

29 Oct 2019

Eva turns five.

'I did not promise. I getricked you aus.'

20 Nov 2019

'Look, papa! It's an old pony but I actually made it a normàl pony, not so old.' 'How did you do that?' 'Put glitter on him!... on her!... Papa, it's a girl pony.'

30 Nov 2019

Eva: 'You don't respect me! You need to respect me!' Me, astounded: 'Is this because I said you have to eat lunch to have dessert?' 'Yes! You don't respect me at all.' (I think this was all in English but am not certain.)

30 No, 2019

Emma turns eleven.

A new toy craze. Eva: 'I'm wünsching me... mmm... Ich wünsche mir Slime!' (I want Slime.)

4 Dec 2019

Emma, proudly: 'It's glitter slime that farts. I made it myself.'

7 Jan 2020

More Germlish (or Denglisch, as it is called in German), by Eva: 'I'm schwitzing', from *schwitzen*, to sweat. 'Papa, you have to schmeiss this weg', from *wegschmeissen,* to throw away.

22 Jan 2020

'Emma, where's Ireland?' 'Near the North Pole.' Seeing my consternation. 'South Pole?' Quickly. 'In Grönland!'

25 Jan 2020

Eva, angry: 'You are my not cool father! You have a cool mama: babushka. But I have no cool papa. You are not cool.'

10 Feb 2020

I'm in the kitchen, Emma and Eva are playing really nicely in the other room. Emma is telling Eva a story. Suddenly I hear a *howl*. I run. It's Eva. She was in some competition in Emma's story and she got *second* place. She howls for *forty-five* minutes. Nothing I do is of any avail. She is screaming so loud it's unbearable. And crying and hitting. Meanwhile Emma takes advantage of the chaos and starts playing video games. When it all ends and Emma and I are outside, I am like, 'Why couldn't you give her first place in your story?!' Emma: 'Because she was competing for the first time!'

22 Feb 2020

'Where's the straw?' Eva: 'You have to suche it' [suchen = to search]. 'I can't find it!... Wait, what are you doing?' Eva, climbing on the sink: 'Suching the straw!'

1 Mar 2020

'I putzed my nose and then I stolpert over the Hocker.'

putzen = to clean
stolpern = to trip, stumble
der Hocker = stool

1 Mar 2020

Emma: 'Papa!' Me: 'What?' 'Not you.' 'You have a different papa?' 'We're playing a game that we're dinosaurs. (dismissively) Eva's idea... (thoughtfully) Although dinosaurs don't usually ride skateboards', as she rides past my door on a skateboard.

14 Mar 2020

'Papa, hide! I'll count to fifty!' 'You can count to fifty?!' 'Wo ist... What is fifty?' I open up my hands five times. 'Hmm... I'll count to twelve.'

4 Apr 2020

Eva saunters into the kitchen in a pink lace number with a pink hairband, climbs into her highchair, downs a chocolate milk, and asks, reclining while eating a mango with a toothpick: 'Why... is there men?' Emma starts explaining the Facts of Life. Eva, distrustfully: 'Vielleicht!'

vielleicht = maybe

18 Apr 2020

These are some of the things my daughters said when they were little. I tried to write them down as quickly and exactly as I could. I was fascinated not only by their formation as speaking subjects and by the poetic and philosophical creativity that accompanied the process, but also by how they mixed languages, often in the same phrase, sometimes in the same word. I spoke English with them, whereas my wife spoke German (although our own childhood languages, Russian and Turkish respectively, also made rare appearances). The older daughter spent much of her first four-and-a-half years in New York, but the younger one was born after we moved to Berlin. I posted our daughters' sayings on closed social media accounts, in order that friends and relatives in different countries might get an impression of their personalities.

Keeping records let me witness not only childhood language development but also early bilingualism. Astonishingly, their language mixing was neither random nor undertaken for emphasis. It was grammatical. Especially the younger daughter would speak to me in an English whose verbs were in German, although they often had English endings. I was shocked that she instinctively knew which word was a verb and which wasn't, and which part of the verb was the root, and which the suffix. Surely my surprise was naive, but I'm not a child-language specialist. When I ask my university first-years to find the main verb in a sentence, many cannot (although this must be because I am asking them to make conscious what they presumably do unconsciously... at least I hope so).

While morphology and syntax appeared built-in, logical thinking took much longer to take hold. When my older daughter was at the linguistically savvy age of almost four, I tried to explain to her that moving to the *next* natural number was the same as adding one – and failed miserably. But sometime later it clicked and became 'self-evident'. At the same age, the syllogistic arguments I made to my younger daughter repeatedly failed to work. Even when she did not have an obvious stake in the outcome, she could admit their formal validity but deny their truth in life. Again, being a total novice in child development, I could not help seeing the rationalist basis of European and Islamic philosophy, founded on the definition of the human being as a rational animal, fall apart right in front of me. If the reader wants to say *duh,* now is a good time to do it.

I was learning a lot about poetry and philosophy from my daughters. Or rather, I was learning a lot about *how to do* poetry and philosophy. In poetry as I understand it, one must play with words and also constantly question them – and do so in a way that is emotionally resonant, that is to say: existentially relevant. Philosophy, as I understand it, reflects on how we use words and larger linguistic structures (and other sign structures) to model the world. Both of these types of linguistic behaviour are characteristic of children but greatly restricted in adults. This too is a cliché – a modernist cliché, as a matter of fact – but a cliché lived is a cliché understood.

I was also learning a lot about bilingualism. I was learning that communicative rules are local and *ad hoc,* adjusting themselves according to situation. I was learning that the ideal of linguistic purity advocated by many poets is effective only in some situations but not for all of them. (A bit of reading shows the historical connection between that monolingual ideal and the emergence of the nation state as a community of speakers of a particular 'native tongue', which renders any kind of cross-linguistic influence – and the fact of childhood bilingualism – a challenge to nationalism.) Moreover, I felt validated as a poet whose writing systematically draws on interlingual and intralingual puns. My children's spectacular word play, such as 'Don Quixote – Donkey Hotty' and 'Verbliud – Wer... blutige', proved that associating words by their materiality was not some display of educational elitism but, on the contrary, the natural and default setting for the linguistic behaviour of somebody who grew up with more than one language. I learned that punning – certainly interlingual but, by force of habit, also intralingual – can function in many situations as a gesture of personal and transnational liberation.

Before trying to publish these sayings, I sought permission from the authors, which was kindly granted. I then asked them if they wanted me to keep their names as they are or to change them. The older, who is now sixteen, requested that her name be changed to something more common and less identifiable. So, together, we decided on Emma. But the younger, who is now ten, wanted me to refer to her under her real name, Eva, because, as she explained, 'I want to be famous'.

Poems

CIHAD HAMMY

War

On the table, I unfolded
the pages of *Macbeth*.

Ink glistening on a notebook.
Half-full glass of tea,
steam deserting,

unrequitedly.
I stared at the jasmines,
odourless, before me.

The journalist reporting
about my city live on TV

is cut mid-sentence
by the blackout.

With my shoes on
the wrong feet, elegantly,

I pocket my keys,
depart my apartment.

Swimming in the fog
of war, I lost my address.

Boat People

Boat is stamped
on the people as a forename.

In the middle of the sea,
the boat dupes the people,

detaching itself beneath
their feet in the jaws
of berserk waves.

The boat
sails without a surname.

Lightened from the burden
of the forename,

the people shut their eyes.

Basketball Hall

In the basketball court,
hundreds of beds

above the white spittle
of yesterday's players. I fall

asleep, eyes wide open.

The next day, they take me
to be scanned,

reconnoiter my body,
sidestepping terrains of pain.

Documenting my weight
on paper, not a care

for what might be broken
by the weight of the way

that lay behind me.
I am driven back to the court.

A black woman scrubs
at the white spit stains.

I close my eyes on a bed, woken
by her scrubbing sounds.

Dublin Treaty

On the Hungarian border,
the stark scent of barbecue
filled my nose.
My gut chased after the smell
into the wood.
In the smoky haze,
I saw people burning
their fingerprints
to leapfrog the Dublin treaty.

Guests Revisited

A wooden camp
houses my sick brother

and me. An orphaned
space, its façade bulged

by rotting fungi, timber,
foul microns soaring

away. A mouse hole
for a room, its dark walls

etched with Turkish,
Serbian, Greek, Italian, –

scrawls of boredom
and desperation,

distant lovers' names,
The Beloved, grown now

overgrown in the heart.
'This was a place

for guest workers,'
the deadpan German

informed us with
commensurate flatness.

'Now, it's yours!'

Memory's Myriad

I check social media to see
if my old friends still drink water.

Do they still kiss life?
Do they borrow from Brutus

to stab childhood friends?
Do they stretch the prison walls

with freedom's warble?

Do they greet the Mediterranean
depths and its sinking

pale cadavers?

Or stare beyond fences to free
memory from camp confines?

Or sweat-bathe together

in basement boiler rooms?
Their compass lost or broken

in the forest's labyrinth?
War's venal shadow distracts

my search. Military checkpoints
interrogate all queries.

I search for our photos,
when we were trapped under

the echo of the bombs.

Those persisting images
from my surviving album –

my imperfect memory –
still, I long to be with them.

Some Contributors

Andrew Biswell is general editor of the collected works of Anthony Burgess. His publications include *Obscenity and the Arts* (2018) and *A Shorter Ulysses* (forthcoming in 2025).

Angela Leighton has published six volumes of poetry, among them *Spills* (2016), recalling her Italian-English background, and most recently *Something, I Forget* (2023).

Anthony Rudolf's next book is his fifth and final memoir, *In the Picture: Office Hours at the Studio of Paula Rego*.

Armand D'Angour is a Professor of Classics at the University of Oxford. He recently published *How to Talk about Love: an Ancient Guide for Modern Lovers* (2026).

Cihad Hammy is a Kurd from Kobani, Syria. In 2015, he took the perilous journey to Germany to continue his education. He is currently pursuing a Master's degree in English and American Literature at the University of Hamburg.

Doaa Kaddah is a third-year PhD candidate in Social Cultural Anthropology at the Freie University of Berlin. Her dissertation, *Colonial Echoes and Transformative Subjectivities: Mapping Maadi's Complex Landscapes in Egypt's New Republic*, examines how colonial histories remain present in urban spaces and daily life, using the Cairo neighbourhood of Maadi as a case study. Now based in Berlin, she continues to explore the ways personal and collective histories intertwine within the spaces we inhabit.

Eugene Ostashevsky is an American poet and translator born in Leningrad. He is the author of *The Feeling Sonnets* (Carcanet, 2022) and *The Pirate Who Does Not Know the Value of Pi* (NYRB, 2022).

Howard Cooper is a rabbinic graduate of the Leo Baeck College, a psychoanalyst in private practice, and the Director of Spiritual Development at Finchley Reform Synagogue, London. He is an author with a particular interest in the intersection of literature, psychoanalysis and spirituality. He blogs intermittently at https://hcooper1146.edublogs.org

Isobel Williams wrote and illustrated *The Supreme Court: A Guide for Bears* (2017), *Catullus: Shibari Carmina* (2021) and *Switch: The Complete Catullus* (Carcanet Classics, 2023).

Jane Duran's most recent collection is *the clarity of distant things* (Carcanet 2021). She and Gloria García Lorca have translated Lorca's *Gypsy Ballads* (Enitharmon 2011) and his *Sonnets of Dark Love* and *The Tamarit Divan* (2017).

Kirsty Gunn's latest collection of short stories, *Pretty Ugly*, is a form of double-speech, bringing the Scottish and New Zealand 'sides' of her childhood together at last.

Marilyn Hacker is the author of nineteen books of poetry, including *Calligraphies* (Norton, 2023) and *Blazons* (Carcanet, 2019), and translator of twenty-two books by French and Francophone poets.

Miles Burrows was born in Leicester. He studied Russian in National Service, then Classics and Medicine at Oxford. He reviewed for the *New Statesman*, and worked as a doctor in New Guinea, Thailand and Taiwan. His poems are published by Cape and Carcanet and in several anthologies.

Oksana Maksymchuk is a bilingual Ukrainian-American poet, scholar and translator. Her English-language debut *Still City: Diary of an Invasion* (Carcanet Press, 2024) is her third collection of poetry.

Parwana Fayyaz is an assistant professor at the Department of Middle Eastern and South Asian Languages and Cultures at the University of Virginia. She earned a BA and MA in Comparative Literature and Creative Writing at Stanford and a PhD at Trinity College, Cambridge. She was a Fellow of Peterhouse from 2020 to 2024.

Peter Davidson is Senior Research Fellow at Campion Hall, University of Oxford, where he is also responsible for the Hall's collections of paintings and furniture. He is the author of *Arctic Elegies, Distance and Memory, Poems of St Robert Southwell, The Palace of Oblivion*, all published by Carcanet.

Philip Terry was born in Belfast, and is a poet and translator. *The Penguin Book of Oulipo,* which he edited, was published in Penguin Modern Classics in 2020, and Carcanet published his edition of Jean-Luc Champerret's *The Lascaux Notebooks*, the first ever anthology of Ice Age poetry, in 2022. His version of *Dante's Purgatorio*, relocated to Mersea Island in Essex, was published by Carcanet in October 2024.

Rahul Soni is a writer, editor and translator. He has translated books of poetry and fiction, including Geetanjali Shree's novel *The Roof Beneath Their Feet* (forthcoming from And Other Stories in 2026).

Shrikant Verma (1931–1986) was a central figure in the *Nai Kavita* literary movement. He published books of fiction, a travelogue, essays and five collections of poetry.e

Sinéad Morrissey is the author of six poetry collections and a Professor of Creative Writing at Newcastle University. Her memoir *Among Communists* will be published by Carcanet in March 2026.

Sir Michael Edwards is poet writing in English and in French. His most recent books in English, *At the Brasserie Lipp* and *Another Art of Poetry and Doorstones*, are published by Carcanet. He is a member of the Académie française.

Stav Poleg's debut poetry collection *The City* is published by Carcanet (2022). It was chosen for the *Financial Times'* Best Summer Books 2022, and was shortlisted for the Seamus Heaney Poetry Prize for a First Collection, 2023. Her poetry has appeared on both sides of the *Atlantic*, in the *New Yorker*, Poetry Daily, *Poetry Ireland Review*, *PN Review* and elsewhere. Her second poetry collection, *The Banquet*, is forthcoming from Carcanet in Autumn 2025.

Thomas A Clark's *the threadbare coat (selected poems)* and *that which appears,* are available from Carcanet. A new book, *thrums,* also from Carcanet, will be published in the autumn.

Victoria Moul is a scholar, translator and poet living in Paris.

Zinovy Zinik was born in Moscow, USSR, and has been living in London since the mid-70s, contributing to the BBC and the *TLS*. His books of fiction include *The Mushroom Picker* (1987), *Sounds Familiar* (2016) and a collection of selected stories in Russian, *No Cause for Alarm* (2022).

WWWW.PNREVIEW.CO.UK

Editors
Michael Schmidt
John McAuliffe

Editorial Manager
Andrew Latimer

Contributing Editors
Anthony Vahni Capildeo
Sasha Dugdale
Will Harris

Copyeditor
Maren Meinhardt

Designed by
Andrew Latimer

Editorial address
The Editors at the address on the right. Manuscripts cannot be returned unless accomp anied by a stamped addressed envelope or international reply coupon.

Trade distributors
Combined Book Services Ltd

Represented by
Compass IPS Ltd

Copyright

ISBN 978 1 80017 473 3
ISBN 0144-7076

Subscriptions—6 issues
INDIVIDUAL–print and digital: £45; abroad £65
INSTITUTIONS–print only: £140; abroad £162
INSTITUTIONS–digital only: from Exact Editions (https://shop.exacteditions.com/gb/pn-review)
to: PN Review, Main Library, University of Manchester, Oxford Road, Manchester, M13 9PP, UK

Subscriptions & Enquiries:
support@pnreview.co.uk

Supported by
Supported using public funding by ARTS COUNCIL ENGLAND